Ploductivity

Ploductivity

A PRACTICAL THEOLOGY
OF WORK AND WEALTH

Douglas Wilson

canonpress
Moscow, Idaho

Published by Canon Press
P.O. Box 8729, Moscow, ID 83843
800.488.2034 | www.canonpress.com

Douglas Wilson, *Ploductivity: A Practical Theology of Work and Wealth*
Copyright © 2020 by Douglas Wilson.

Cover design by James Engerbretson.
Interior design by Laura Storm and James Engerbretson.
Printed in the United States of America.

Library of Congress Cataloging-in-Publication Data is forthcoming.

20 21 22 23 24 25 26 27   9 8 7 6 5 4 3 2

CONTENTS

FOREWORD

I'm sure that you, like me, have seen those commercials (probably playing on the TV in a hotel buffet as you stand waiting for your waffle to finish cooking and are therefore a captive audience) in which some generous soul with a lavish lifestyle is offering to sell you a quick and easy road to wealth. "Just buy my book to unlock the secrets that launched me to where I am today!" As far as I can make out, these people made their money by selling people the secret to making money . . . and thus I've often wondered just how informative those books would really turn out to be. Would that author have any tried-and-tested ideas—outside of recommending that I launch my own Get Rich Quick scam?

This is a question I have also had about various productivity gurus. Have they ever accomplished anything productive outside of telling people how to be productive? Sure they're efficient—at selling people efficiency. Sure they've built a brand—but it's a productivity brand. Have they ever built anything else? It can all start to feel a bit small and sad and self-referential.

This book you have in your hand is the opposite of all that in almost every way.

Since Douglas Wilson is my father, I have had a front row seat throughout my entire life and can testify that you will never meet a more productive or fruitful man. And this is quite astonishing if you know him because he is never in a fluster. Never scurrying about in a panic trying to meet the deadlines and reduce the margins and leverage the capital and drive the revenue and slash redundancies and bloviate the expenditures. Or whatever.

On the other hand, he never wastes a minute, and I mean that quite literally. When it comes to the time in his day, he uses every single part of the buffalo. If you happen to see him sitting in his truck at a red light, do not expect a honk and a wave. He won't see you, because he is listening with his full attention to an audio book on his (three minute) commute to work. He'll pick it up again on his (three minute) commute home. And he'll get through *War and Peace* by Christmas that way. Back when I was a kid and Audible wasn't a thing and there wasn't even a cassette player in his truck, his solo drives would involve stopping at a stop light, picking up the book next to him on the seat and reading. He definitely wouldn't wave to you as you crossed the crosswalk in front of him because he'd be highlighting something with his blue high-lighter, book open on the steering wheel.

Patience—with a bomb shot of ambition, or possibly ambition that is ruled and tempered by patience—is the surprisingly powerful combination that has made his work so unbelievably fruitful. I've watched him build a house from the ground up—on evenings and Saturdays. I've watched him launch a successful magazine out of a church newsletter that we kids would stuff and label once a month on Saturday mornings, paid in donuts. I've seen him build a completely innovative and visionary school so that his children could be given an education that he himself never received. I remember him taking classes at the local university to learn Latin—because he wanted his children to learn but there weren't any Latin teachers. In the early years of the school, I remember him coming into the school that met in a church basement to teach Latin to a class of 4th graders . . . and then heading out to sit in his truck in the parking lot to work until it was time to head back in to teach again (probably Bible to the 5th graders). In the winter he'd just sit out there and work with the engine on. I've watched him play the long game—and I've seen his patient and faithful and unglamorous work in that school inspire the powerful and game changing national movement that is classical education. I've watched hundreds of schools launch in response to his pioneering work, and the Association of Classical Christian Schools (now with 50,000 students) grow off of our dining room table.

I remember when I said how desperately I didn't want to attend our local state university, he responded with, "What if we started a college?" And such was the uniqueness of my upbringing that it didn't occur to me for a moment that this was an unusual sort of an idea. It sounded great to me. I trusted implicitly that it would magically come together—and it did. It wasn't until much later that I reflected that most high school girls don't have dads who will just whip up a college before their freshman year—particularly not a successful one.

I've watched him take a hippie, Jesus People church that met in a body shop to a large, thriving, spiritually healthy congregation—and from there start a whole denomination.

I've watched the amazing amount of reading he gets in—finishing at least a book a week for at least the last 40 years. At some point along the line he decided to be an author—and I've long since given up trying to keep track of new books he's writing. You just accept the fact that there will be regular new book announcements that you never had any idea he was writing . . . it totals over 100 at this point, as well as countless articles and blog posts. An accurate and up-to-the-minute CV seems to me a logistical impossibility.

But one of the most impressive things I can say about him is that he has never been too busy for his kids. Growing up, he always had a book in his hand—but whenever we wandered out and said, "Hey Dad . . ." he would always immediately set his book down and give us his full attention. When we now crash his evenings on a regular basis for a chat, he always sets aside whatever it is he's working on and will pick it up again after we leave.

The man is endlessly patient, endlessly diligent, shockingly ambitious, and never in a flurry. So when he says he's going to talk about productivity, I would highly recommend that we all listen up.

Rebekah Merkle
November 2019

PART ONE

A THEOLOGY OF
PRODUCTIVITY

AN INTRODUCTION TO TECHNOFULNESS

Is it possible for someone to be both relaxed *and* driven? People who are only relaxed are frequently slackers, and much of the book of Proverbs would appear to apply to them. But people who are driven give a diligent work ethic a bad name. Nobody wants to be like that. We might admire the house they can afford, but no one wants to be like the people who live in it.

This is a book about personal productivity, and I trust that about halfway through this we will get to the point where we can discuss it productively. But before getting to the actual subject at hand, which we will do in the second portion of the book, it is necessary to clear away a good bit of debris. Unless we do it this way, we run an extreme risk of failing to distinguish between efficiency and effectiveness. As Peter Drucker said, "*Efficiency* is doing things right; *effectiveness* is doing the right things."

It is not possible to bring up the subject of productivity without summoning up a number of nearly invisible background metaphors. They can vary somewhat between different readers, but because we all live in the shared space that modernity provides for us, those background metaphors will have a lot in common: they will all owe much to the Industrial Revolution.

Who wants to be a well-oiled cog in the machine? Who wants to increase their measurable outputs? Who wants to shave minutes off their scheduled routines? These questions are the kind of questions that efficiency experts might raise after their visit to the factory. But do you want to be efficient like a machine, or fruitful like a tree?

When a man buys a book on personal productivity like this, it is likely he already has a vision in his mind of what success looks like. But where did he get that vision? He is probably thirsting after the next life hack, the next hot tip, the three steps to an empty inbox, and so on. People who buy books on productivity are frequently junkies who are lusting after a new technique or trick. And once a technique is implemented for a few weeks, the book goes on the shelf with all the others, like a piece of exercise equipment in a garage full of exercise equipment.

But I sincerely hope, at least for a number of you readers, this will be the last productivity book you read. *Not* because I have discovered the Lost Technique that once made Atlantis great and which I am about to share with you all for a modest fee, but rather because I hope this book will help you deal with the issues surrounding productivity in such a way as to help you mortify that most peculiar lust.

8

This relates to the matter of the admittedly odd title of this first chapter—*An Introduction to Technofulness*. And since the name will have to be explained at some point, why not now? In this book, I am seeking to stake out an entirely different third position, over against the twin errors of *technophobia* and *technophilia*.

The technophile is the early and eager adapter. He tries *everything* out, and subscribes to magazines and web digests that help him try everything out. He is the guy waiting overnight on the sidewalk for the latest iPhone release. He can't wait until some tech giant develops a thumb drive for the base of his skull that will give him instant fluency in Spanish. He is urging Google on in their pursuit of their version of everlasting life, where they will upload his digital consciousness to the cloud. It does not occur to him that he is simply yearning to become an old-fashioned ghost, haunting the computers of his old co-workers and weirded-out family members.

The technophobe is not *quite* the opposite. He rarely wants to go back to pre-Sumerian scratch, preferring instead to draw an arbitrary line with regard to the recent history of technological development. Past that capricious line he refuses to feel comfortable. The Amish drew the line sometime in the 19th century—technological development up to that point was somehow legit, but past that point it mysteriously ceased to be so. Their reaction seems both quaint and odd to us, but we should remember that there was a time when horseless carriages and locomotives were as mind-bending to their generation as cybernetics, nanotechnology, and robotics are to ours. The unknown or unusual can certainly scare us, but being scared by something new is not a theology. We need something more than that.

If we get the theology of the thing right, then it should be something that our great-grandchildren can apply fruitfully fifty years from now when they are trying to incorporate *who-knows-what* into their daily lives. It probably won't be the iPhone 92.

In the meantime, Wendell Berry's wife types his manuscripts on a Royal Standard typewriter. No computer. Not using a computer to write a book involves unusual levels of purity rarely seen in these corrupt times. The computers that go into manufacturing his books don't get into the act until *after* the manuscript arrives at the publisher and somebody scans it into the system. However, what I have failed to grasp in all this is why Royal Standard typewriters have been allowed to squeeze out the quill pen.

We have a perennial temptation to locate sin as resident in the *stuff*. Some refuse to see sin in the stuff, and therefore conclude that there must not be any sin. These are the technophiles. Others see clearly that there *is* sin, and so they conclude that it must be in the stuff, though maybe it is not in the *earlier* stuff. These are the technophobes.

But there is a third option. Plenty of sin accompanies technology, just as plenty of sin accompanies lack of technology. However, the basic driving problem is always in the human heart, always in our *use* of technology, and that use is shaped and driven by our attitudes about it. Maxwell's silver hammer did come down upon somebody's head, but we go astray when we blame the silver hammer. The problem was in Maxwell.

Now, what we call technology is simply an array of tools laid out on the bench for us. *Technology is therefore a form of wealth.* The reason this is important is because the Bible says very little about technology as such, but it gives us a great deal of blunt and pointed teaching on the subject of wealth. If we learn how to deal with *wealth* scripturally, then we will have learned how to deal with technology.

This also makes it obvious that these problems are not new problems at all. Something Solomon insisted on, and that we ignore to our own detriment in matters of technology, is that there is nothing new under the sun. We assume because we are in new territory—uncharted territory—we don't have to look to the Bible for our direction. But if it is a perennial problem, then the Bible probably talks about it. We are *not* in uncharted territory.

So if technology is wealth, then we are all surrounded with astounding amounts of it. This is what I refer to as *tangible grace.* If you have a smartphone, you have more wealth in your pocket than Nebuchadnezzar accumulated over the course of his lifetime. We have responsibility to turn a profit on these astounding resources—and that is what is meant by *productivity.* We have a responsibility to do this methodically, deliberately, and intentionally. This is what I mean by *ploductivity.* This is deliberate faithfulness: working in the same direction over an extended period of time. Our electronic servants may be super fast, but we should be as deliberate as ever.

When the Bible was written, society was agrarian. There were no smartphones. No helicopters. "You can't expect us to find answers for these, our postmodern times, in that glaringly pre-modern book." But that is precisely what we *should* expect. The Scriptures speak to our condition, and because we are wealthy, they speak to it very directly. But we have to be prepared to listen.

CHAPTER ONE

A THEOLOGY
OF WORK

One of the first things we must recognize is that work does not exist in the world because of the Fall. Work got a lot more *difficult* because of our sin, and we do labor under the ramifications of a curse. But God gave the cultural mandate to mankind, a mandate which involved an enormous amount of work, *before* the entrance of sin. Not only so, but that same cultural mandate is reiterated to Noah, right after the Flood, which means that the presence of sin has not altered the mission (Gen. 9:1). We therefore need to recover a distinctively Christian work ethic as an essential part of the process of salvation and sanctification. It points, like every faithful thing does, to Christ, and in Christ all of these issues are connected.

Work is related to tools, and tools are related to productivity. If we want to get it right, we therefore need a theology of work, a theology of tools, and a theology of productivity.

"Seest thou a man diligent in his business? He shall stand before kings; He shall not stand before mean men" (Prov. 22:29).

The King James rendering of "mean men" does not intend unkind or cruel men, but rather obscure or contemptible men. The ESV renders it this way: "Do you see a man skillful in his work? He will stand before kings; he will not stand before obscure men" (Prov. 22:29). Solomon is saying that first-rate work is going to be recognized.

So as we will see in a number of texts from Proverbs, work has consequences. Laziness also has consequences, because God gave us the ultimate "gold standard" called time, and everyone has exactly the same amount of it. It is a resource that the government cannot print. This means that *work over time* matters, and *no work over time* matters. When I say that it *matters*, I mean that it matters in morally significant ways. You can, and should, draw conclusions about people based on their work. Our ability to evaluate the labor of others is not absolute because we are limited and finite. Our judgments should be made in all humility. But this does not alter the fact that we still need to evaluate others, and an important part of that evaluation includes the quality of their work.

This is why the Scriptures say, "He also that is slothful in his work is brother to him that is a great waster" (Prov. 18:9). Laziness is a destroyer. But how can it be, when it didn't touch anything, when it didn't consume anything? The problem is that it *did* consume something—it burned a lot of daylight.

In the text mentioned above, a man is set before us, a man who is diligent in his business. The word for diligent is *ma-hir*—experienced, skilled. Do you see a man who is on top

14

of his vocation? The word rendered *business* is a broad term, and trade, craftsmanship, and wares are all included. *That* man will stand before kings. This is simply Solomon's way of saying that cream rises to the top.

Taking one thing with another, all things considered, diligence is recognized and honored in the world, and laziness is recognized and shunned. This understanding collides with a common Christian misconception of grace and works. Because we are saved by grace—and we *are*—we sometimes assume that the world is God's welfare state, and that all the other Christians owe us ecclesiastical food stamps. When we don't get them, there are "hurt Christian feelings."

Christians are involved in building community, which means that we do business with one another. So one of our great challenges is the "cheap grace" approach to work, the one that constantly argues that "Christians aren't perfect, just forgiven."

What is the result of this attitude? Contractors who don't come close to their estimate or deadline. Wives who manipulate their husbands into doing half their work for them. Husbands who fail to provide wives with the wherewithal to do their work. Students who dither at their assignments. Entrepreneurs who risk all the wrong things. Web designers who flake. Buyers who write and sign contracts they don't know how to read. Sellers who don't write contracts at all, on the assumption that regeneration somehow makes everyone's memories perfect. And so on.

And in case any of this stepped on any toes, there is *no solidarity* between a competent contractor and an incompetent one, or a competent wife and an incompetent one. True

Christian fellowship and camaraderie should exist between an outstanding web designer and an outstanding architect, in a way that does not exist between a great architect and a lazy one. This is because cream rises. *We must learn to draw the lines of solidarity in the right places.* Shared honesty across professions is a sound basis of solidarity. A shared profession, with some who are honest and others who are scoundrels, is not.

Honest members of a Christian community must learn that job evaluation is not gossip. It is part of the cost of doing business, and so we have to learn how to provide honest feedback without quarreling, and that feedback must not be fanatically over-precise, and neither may it inflict a terrible craftsman on the next unsuspecting saint. If you get together with a friend and talk about how so-and-so is having trouble in his marriage, and you are not part of the solution, then you are part of the problem. You *are* a gossip. But if you tell a friend who asked about it that your brother in Christ installed your kitchen cabinets upside down, that is *not* gossip. People who do not want public evaluation of the quality of their work are people who have no business being in business. They should just buy a shovel and dig where they are told to.

This point about solidarity is an important one. Those who are walking in honesty have unity in that honesty. Those who drift in their slackness have unity in that drift. But one of the ways that people try to keep pointed exhortations at bay is by misconstruing the point of the exhortation. One of the things we learn from Proverbs is that slipshod approaches to work and lame excuses go together. If we are confronting problems that we have with regard to work, we need to be prepared for some misdirection in response.

Suppose I preached a sermon about stealing stereos. Smith has a stereo he bought and paid for. Murphy stole his stereo. The sermon is not about *having* a stereo. It is about stealing them. And so if Smith comes to see me with tears in his eyes and offers to show me the receipt, he has missed the point. And if Murphy attacks me for my bias against stereo ownership, he is diligently *trying* to miss the point. If this seems obscure, let me put it into real terms. Suppose I use as a sermon illustration the tendency of contractors to overpromise and under-deliver, with regard to both costs and timelines. Smith is the contractor who feels bad after the sermon, even though he has never done that, but he feels bad simply because he is a *contractor*. Murphy does that all the time, and criticizes the sermon because I obviously have it in for contractors. Both are missing the point.

So good work matters, but what does good work look like?

First, work is a good thing, and the hard way is actually the easy way. As a general rule, the difficult parts should be moved to the front of the project. There is a way of avoiding work that multiplies work, and there is a way of embracing-work that saves work in the long run. "The way of the slothful man is as an hedge of thorns: But the way of the righteous is made plain" (Prov. 15:19). As the saying goes, if you don't have time to do it right, then how will you have time to do it over?

Second, the right kind of work—when a particular result is desired—quenches the wrong kind of desire. "A worker's appetite works for him; his mouth urges him on" (Prov. 16:26, ESV). Men hustle when they're hungry, and a refusal to work inflames the wrong kind of desire. "The soul of the sluggard desireth, and hath nothing: But the soul of the diligent shall be made fat" (Prov. 13:4). Not having a job means that he can think about that flat screen television that he wants so much, and he can think about it all day long. "The desire of the slothful killeth him; For his hands refuse to labour. He coveteth greedily all the day long: But the righteous giveth and spareth not" (Prov. 21:25–26). Workers are generous. Loafers are not.

Third, the Bible teaches that diligence and laziness are *visible*. Professionalism begins in the heart, but it does not remain there: "He becometh poor that dealeth with a slack hand: But the hand of the diligent maketh rich. He that gathereth in summer is a wise son: But he that sleepeth in harvest is a son that causeth shame" (Prov. 10:4–5). Put another way, the lazy son is not being lazy in his heart. He is being lazy in the *harvest*.

Fourth, the diligent like to have their work speak for them, and unproductive men like to substitute talk for action. Lazy men are good talkers. "In all labour there is profit: But the talk of the lips tendeth only to penury" (Prov. 14:23).

Part of the reason that the lazy man is verbally adept is that he has to be ready with excuses. They are on the tip of his tongue. "Can you believe it? My software updated on me in the final paragraph and I had to start over from scratch." Or, "Aliens kidnapped me. What year is it?" Or, "The slothful man saith, There is a lion in the way; A lion is in the streets. As the door turneth upon his hinges, So doth the slothful upon his bed. The slothful hideth his hand in his bosom; It grieveth him to bring it again to his mouth. The sluggard is wiser in his own conceit than seven men that can render a reason" (Prov. 26:13–16).

Certain functionaries have been asleep at their desk so long that one side of their head is flat. When they get home they wear themselves out trying to decide between sitting down to do nothing or lying down to do nothing. He digs his hand into the crinkly bag, but the Cheeto is too heavy to get back to his mouth. But he is always ready with an explanation.

We are addressing what our salvation looks like when it comes to work. Remember that proverbs are *proverbs*, and that they do not give us truths about triangles having three sides. But they are still true, overwhelmingly true. And the book of Proverbs talks about laziness and work a *lot*. We may be justified in thinking that it is a perennial problem.

> I went by the field of the slothful, And by the vineyard of the man void of understanding; And, lo, it was all grown over with thorns, And nettles had covered the face thereof, And the stone wall thereof was broken down. Then I saw, and considered it well: I looked upon it, and received instruction. Yet a little sleep, a little slumber, A little folding of the hands to sleep: So shall thy poverty come as one that travelleth; And thy want as an armed man. (Prov. 24:30–34)

The issue is not whether we are saved by works. Of course not. The issue here, rather, is what salvation *looks* like. We are saved by grace, but *grace works*. "Work out your own salvation with fear and trembling, for it is God who works in you, both to will and to work for his good pleasure" (Phil. 2:12–13, ESV).

We are not saved *by* good works (Eph. 2:8-9), but we are saved *to* good works (Eph. 2:10). Immediately after this famous verse where Paul says we are saved by grace through faith, he then says that we are God's workmanship, created in Christ Jesus for good works, which God prepared beforehand for us to do. This salvation by grace is a salvation unto good works.

In our sin, we were a bad work. The grace of God picked us up and placed us on God's work bench, where He made us His project. The word there is *poiema*, which means creation or work—we are God's craftsmanship. He fashioned us into the kind of creatures who are able to *do good work*. Our good works are never at the front end, but they most certainly are at the back end.

Work is not a curse. The curse affects work, but work remains a gift from a gracious God. We were created for work, and we were created for work in an astoundingly fruitful world. In short, the grace of God leads to salvation and salvation leads to good works. As we consider this, we ought not to limit the phrase "good works" to helping little old ladies across the street or volunteering at soup kitchens. Those are included, certainly, but good works also include *good work*. Good works include turning a table leg on a lathe, or solving a mathematical problem, or shoveling out the barn. In sum, good works include, necessarily, the blessing of good work.

CHAPTER TWO

A THEOLOGY OF
WEALTH

In this fallen world, wealth *does* have a bias towards self-sufficiency rather than to dependence on God. But this is not something the wealth does to us, but rather something we do with the wealth. Wealth—monetary, technological, or otherwise—is simply and solely a good thing, a gift of God. The sin enters in when the means of self-sufficiency are placed in the hands of someone who has entirely the wrong attitude about autonomous self-sufficiency.

To say that wealth has a bias to self-sufficiency is a figure of speech. Wealth is inanimate, and it has no thoughts on the matter at all, one way or another. Wealth doesn't care—the diamonds don't care, the gold doesn't care, the stock portfolio doesn't care, all the tools on your workbench don't care. And when I say they don't care, I mean they don't care whether you sin with them or not. To say that wealth has a bias is really to say that men and women have a bias when we look at them in relationship with the wealth around them.

Here is how the problem is described in Deuteronomy:

> When thou hast eaten and art full, then thou shalt bless the LORD thy God for the good land which he hath given thee. Beware that thou forget not the LORD thy God, in not keeping his commandments, and his judgments, and his statutes, which I command thee this day: Lest when thou hast eaten and art full, and hast built goodly houses, and dwelt therein; And when thy herds and thy flocks multiply, and thy silver and thy gold is multiplied, and all that thou hast is multiplied; Then thine heart be lifted up, and thou forget the LORD thy God, which brought thee forth out of the land of Egypt, from the house of bondage . . . And thou say in thine heart, My power and the might of mine hand hath gotten me this wealth. But thou shalt remember the LORD thy God: for it is he that giveth thee power to get wealth, that he may establish his covenant which he sware unto thy fathers, as it is this day. (Deut. 8:10–18)

Look closely at what the text says here. It says that a host of *good* things are *good* gifts from a *good* God. Full meals, good houses, multiplying flocks and herds, silver and gold multiplying as well, and the same good growth happening to everything else the wealthy possess. All the good comes from outside, from the hand of the Lord.

Where does the bad come from then? Moses warns the wealthy about their *heart* being lifted up. He tells them that they are in danger of forgetting the Lord their God. From that poor beginning, their hearts are lifted up, and they lay claim to the pride of life. They say in their blinded conceit that their own hand was the source of their wealth. Here lies the fundamental mistake, the fundamental problem.

The arrogant human heart is the source of the sin concerning wealth, and the arrogant human heart sins this way in the proximity of wealth. Wealth is not the locus of the sin, but the presence of the wealth is the locus of the temptation. Just as a beautiful woman is not the cause of lust but merely the occasion for it, so also the presence of wealth is not the cause of self-sufficiency. But we see, over and again from Genesis to Revelation, that wealth provides the occasion for the sin of self-sufficiency. As Cotton Mather once put it, "Faithfulness begat prosperity, and the daughter devoured the mother."

But what about the camel and the eye of the needle (Mk. 10:25)? What about the very rich farmers who were ripping off their laborers (Jas. 5:1-6)? What about that famous passage that says that the love of money is the root of all evil (1 Tim. 6:10)? We want to submit ourselves fully and completely to the teaching of such passages, but we have to be careful not to bring our preconceived notions about the essential corruption of the wealth itself into it. Let's take this last warning from 1 Timothy for an example.

> For the love of money is the root of all evil: which while some coveted after, they have erred from the faith, and pierced themselves through with many sorrows . . . Charge them that are rich in this world, that they be not highminded, nor trust in uncertain riches, but in the living God, who giveth us richly all things to enjoy; That they do good, that they be rich

in good works, ready to distribute, willing to communicate; Laying up in store for themselves a good
foundation against the time to come, that they may
lay hold on eternal life. (1 Tim. 6:10, 17–19)

First, when Paul says "all evil," we should keep in mind
that the Greek word *pas* (all), when linked to a noun can be
accurately translated as "all kinds of," as the ESV does in this
place: "For the love of money is a root of *all kinds of evils*. It
is through this craving that some have wandered away from
the faith and pierced themselves with many pangs" (1 Tim.
6:10, ESV).

Second, and more importantly, look closely at what Paul
tells these rich people to do. He tells them to not be snobs,
and not to trust in their wealth, but rather in the living God.
And how is the living God described here? As the one "who
giveth us richly all things *to enjoy*" (v. 17). He tells them to
enjoy what they have, and then tells them to be active in doing good, to be rich in good works, to be generous and eager
to share.

He does not say that being rich is like having cooties, and
that they should be trying to pass their cooties off to somebody else. As I say, he *doesn't* teach that.

Now if my thesis is correct, and if tools and technology
are to be understood as important forms of wealth, then this
gives us the rubric we need for dealing with our tools and our
technology in a biblical manner.

Because thou servedst not the LORD thy God with
joyfulness, and with gladness of heart, for the abundance of all things; Therefore shalt thou serve thine

24

enemies which the LORD shall send against thee, in hunger, and in thirst, and in nakedness, and in want of all things: and he shall put a yoke of iron upon thy neck, until he have destroyed thee. (Deut. 28:47–48)

Notice what we are told here. The solution to self-sufficiency is *not* to banish the goods that we used to forget God, but rather to make a point of remembering God in and through the abundance He gave to us. What was their problem? It was that they did not serve God with joy and gladness *for the abundance.*

We are not only tempted by wealth, we are tempted to *blame* wealth. It can be a sin to misunderstand the nature of sin. In other words, we are tempted to locate the sin in the stuff, and then we try to solve the problem (when and if we do try to solve it) by putting some kind of respectable distance between us and the stuff. If people sin with alcohol, tobacco and firearms, *and they do*, then we think we must regulate the substances (or the tools) themselves.

We do it like this because we can at least (we think) throw the stuff away. It is a physical thing out there, and so it appears that we can distance ourselves from it. But if the problem is in our hearts, *always* in our hearts, whatever shall we do? We can't throw our hearts away. We can't get a new heart, or at least we cannot get a new heart on our own. If I were to make a decision to throw my old heart away, that decision would have to be made by my old heart. And if my old heart could do something as wonderful as throwing my old heart away, what is the need for a new heart?

When we consider the world outside ourselves, it is made up of two realities. The first is the ultimate reality of God, the one who made us, and to whom we are everlastingly in debt. The other reality is creation, which includes all the created order that is external to myself. When I am out of fellowship with God, the only thing available to pursue besides Him is some created bauble. And when I pursue that created thing, trying to get from a finite thing what only the infinite can provide, I have fallen into the vanity of idolatry.

We cannot make the raw material of idolatry go away. God created it, and He is not going to uncreate it for our personal convenience. Rather, God has to give us a heart that is capable of being rightly related to Him in the presence of things that seem to beckon us to be wrongly related to Him. But it only seems that way—the actual beckoning is done when we project our own willful desires onto the blank screen of God's good gifts. A right theology of wealth will equip us to handle tools rightly, doing everything we do to the glory of God.

We normally think of wealth as something that just sits there, like money or stuff. Dollars just sit there in a bank account, and a high-end sofa just sits there in a very nice living room. But wealth is also active—think of investments, for example. I have been emphasizing the wealth that comes in the form of tools, which are designed for activity. Later in this book, we will consider an additional aspect of wealth, which is the fact that it brings a greater ability to summon the labor of others.

So rightly understood, wealth is something you *do*. And that brings us to the next aspect of our study, which is a proper theology of tools.

CHAPTER THREE

A THEOLOGY OF
TOOLS

When God gave the cultural mandate to Adam and Eve, obedience to that mandate could easily have *begun* when they were both naked and unashamed. They could certainly be fruitful and multiply like that. We might consider that as God giving them something of a head start.

But there are other verbs in the cultural mandate (Gen. 1:28). God tells them to replenish the earth, and He also tells them to subdue it. On top of that He commands them to have dominion over the fish, the birds, and every living creature. Quite obviously, one of the first things Adam and Eve were going to need was tools.

Adam could not exercise dominion over a *hedge* without tools, and God told him to exercise dominion over the whole globe and all the animals in it. To exercise dominion over the fish of the sea, I am pretty sure a boat would have been needed. We are told that the descendants of Cain were those who first developed the use of tools. Jubal was the one who invented musical instruments—the lyre and pipes (Gen. 4:21), and Tubal-cain was the inventor of tools fashioned from brass and iron (Gen. 4:22). Also note that this means the development of mining—which requires yet another set of tools. No way were they digging through rock with their bare hands. All these developed during the lifetime of Adam and Eve.

Sometimes people make much of the fact that the tools mentioned were developed in the line of Cain, the bad guy, the one who had gone off and built a *city*, a bad thing, and so we are urged to be appropriately wary of *tools*. In this reckoning, technology has supposedly been our ancient foe.

However, the line of Seth culminates in the deliverance brought about by Noah, and when he built the ark, the use of tools was not optional. This was an enormous technological achievement: the ark was the length of a football field and half as long again. That's half the length of a modern aircraft carrier, and it had to float. And not capsize. In comparison, all the great cities built by Cain and his descendants had this in common: none of them could float. Noah's ark was *the* technological achievement of the antediluvian world. So when it comes to the use of tools, we cannot say that the line of Seth was made up of slouches.

When Noah worked the wood with tools, he was doing the same thing that Jesus did millennia later in his father's shop. And the two of them together were doing the same thing some other carpenter was doing when he fashioned the cross upon which Jesus was going to be crucified. They were all doing the same thing—working with wood—and that thing they were doing tells us nothing about the sinfulness of the activity or not. In order to evaluate a tool, we have to account for the *telos*, the end, the purpose. Hammers are used to build both brothels and barns.

As mentioned before, our perennial temptation is that of locating sin in the stuff. But guns don't kill people, people do. Blocks of stone don't build ziggurats, people do. Gopher wood doesn't build arks, people do.

After the entry of sin into the world, one of the first things that happened was evasion of personal responsibility. Adam blamed the woman for giving him the fruit (and blamed God for giving him the woman), and the woman turned around and blamed the serpent. Sin occurred, and excuses followed hard after.

When we sin with a material object, or in near proximity to a material object, the most obvious thing to occur to us is to blame that material object. We blame weapons for murder, alcohol for drunkenness, slow traffic for the anger, photography for lust, and so on.

Tools can be simple, and they can be sophisticated. When the hammer twists in your hand, and you curse the hammer, you are cursing a very simple tool. When your computer freezes up, and you curse the computer, you are cursing a very complex tool. It is folly in both cases.

So man is not man without tools. The notion that we can be truly human as disembodied and ephemeral spirits is not a Christian idea. We do not believe in the *essential* immortality of the soul, which is the Greek view. Christians believe in the resurrection of the dead. While it is true that our souls *are* immortal, this immortality is a contingent one, dependent upon the grace and goodness of God. And the Creator God, in that grace and goodness, fashioned us as embodied creatures. This is not a design flaw. When God breathed the breath of life into Adam, and Adam first sat up, he did so with two opposable thumbs. And he used one of those thumbs when he chucked his first rock into the first pool he came to.

It is not the case that unbelieving man fanned out into the world in search of hard metals while the descendants of Seth eked out dominion through an adroit use of their fingernails. Notice how the children of Israel hear the land of their inheritance described to them. Not only was it a land flowing with milk and honey, but it was also a land rich in iron and brass.

> For the LORD thy God bringeth thee into a good land, a land of brooks of water, of fountains and depths that spring out of valleys and hills; A land of wheat, and barley, and vines, and fig trees, and pomegranates; a land of oil olive, and honey; A land wherein thou shalt eat bread without scarceness, thou shalt not lack any thing in it; a land whose stones are iron, and out of whose hills thou mayest dig brass. (Deut. 8:7–9)

The world is laden with many good things, and apart from picking an apple or two with your bare hands, any kind of dominion has to be accomplished by means of tools. A man with tools is not being an artificial man. My argument is that a man cannot be an authentic man *without* tools.

Once we have acknowledged this, we find ourselves on a spectrum. Where is the dividing line between the first stick that Adam used to knock down the first bee hive, and the fantastic app you just downloaded to your smartphone earlier today? We can describe the differences, but these differences have to do with traits like simplicity and complexity, and not with whether they are part of a man's body. They are both intended to make a task either possible or easier. Therefore they are both tools. And so we should define a tool in this way: something that is not part of a man's body which makes something that the man wants to do possible or easier.

What tools do is make it possible for a larger number of things to be brought within reach. Either they *extend* your reach, or they bring things *close* to home. At the time of writing, our church offices had recently relocated, which meant that a large majority of my books were packed up in boxes. Of course once the boxes are all stacked and ready to go, the thought occurs to you that there is a conference coming up in a few weeks, and *oh no* maybe some of the books I needed are in the boxes. But my books are cataloged online, and so I went there to hunt for a couple of books, one for the conference and one for a writing project. I typed in the names of the books, and discovered that *both* of them were there within a few feet of where I was sitting. In fact, I could have pulled one of them down without getting out of my chair.

Now of course some might argue that in this case the tool (the computer) was simply subsidizing my incompetence, making it possible for me to function without getting a genuine grip on my immediate surroundings. But I would argue in response that I have a lot of books, and if you have a lot of books, then what you need is a system, and some tools. The tools might be as simple as shelves and ladders, but you still need tools. This tool didn't bring the book close, but it *did* bring knowledge of a close book close.

Just this morning, I took a picture of a couple of depleted products at home and texted the picture to my wife who was on the way to the grocery store. That is an example of extended reach.

Tools enable us to widen our reach. Tools make it possible for our radius of fruitfulness (now *there* is a phrase for the ages) to extend much farther than it otherwise would.

So when Adam found the beehive-knocking-down stick, he was wealthier than he was before. When a man purchases an app for 99 cents, he is wealthier than he was before. Tools are technology, and technology is a form of wealth.

This will be developed more fully as we continue, but what this means is that we should regard our tools the same way we regard our money—with grateful suspicion. Or perhaps, on alternating weeks, with suspicious gratitude. This has to do with the nature of creational goods in a fallen world.

But more about all that in the pages to come.

CHAPTER FOUR

A THEOLOGY OF MEDIA

We are not disembodied souls. We can move around physically and we can bonk into things. This creates enormous theological problems, not to mention occasional bruises.

I am not just my body, either. I am soul, spirit, and body bound all together. But it gets complicated rapidly—because clothes make the man. In a sense, we are continuing our discussion of tools, but there is a bit more than that going on.

Suppose that I decide in my soul that I am going to weed the garden today. In order to reach the garden, in order to make contact with it, I need a bridge—I need a medium. I can't touch it otherwise. In order to connect with my project, whatever it is, I need media—that which enables us to "handle" a world that is distinct from our bodies. The media I use would certainly include my tools, but it would also include my foundational medium, which is to say, my body. So in this chapter, when I refer to media, I am not talking about the news media.

I would define media in this way: working out from and including our bodies, media also include our clothes, other people, and tools, including especially tools for communication and infrastructure.

We see at a glance that a man's hand and the screwdriver in that same hand are distinct realities, but he uses both of them to accomplish things in the world. In fact, he can tighten a screw more effectively with the tool than he could if he tried it "authentically," which is to say, by hand. For tightening a screw, my natural hand is the wrong tool.

What we are grappling with in this chapter is the problem created by media. Man lives in an environment that man has figured out how to manipulate or *use*. When Adam and Eve were first placed in the Garden, they were in an environment but that environment was not yet being used. It was not yet manipulated by media or into media. But that did not take long. Depending on how much time they lived there before the Fall, the Garden would have begun to develop an infrastructure. There would be a plot of ground where they were to grow their food, for example, and a pathway to that plot of ground would begin to develop. And how would Adam till the ground? How would he weed his primal truck patch?

So we have souls, and we have a physical world. God has created us as ensouled physical bodies, and He has given us hands to work with that physical world. But He has also given us handles out there in the physical world. We have bodies, which is why we have hands to go with those handles. Those handles are available, and so we are being positively invited

34

to engage with the world. Much of this is so normal for us that we don't even notice it anymore. This is why most media is invisible to us. We assume that we just happen to have fingernails. We don't reflect on the fact that if we didn't, it would be impossible to pick up a quarter.

Our first parents were clothed to cover the shamefulness of their nakedness, but we do not need to assume that clothes would never have been developed in a world apart from sin. Presumably there would have been some hikes that required shoes, and some temperatures that required warmth, and other occasions which would require majesty and glory. So, working outward, the first line of media would be clothing.

Then we encounter other people. Language was given by God at the very first. Mankind was created as a speaking creature. Adam and Eve could talk as soon as they met each other. In fact, when Adam was introduced to Eve, not only did he immediately speak, he spoke in poetry.

Language is part of this complex world of media. We ought not to be thrown by the fact that we even think using language. And this fact should tell us that we were created for community. We speak and are spoken to, which means that between us and our conversation partner, we are manipulating the air with our teeth, lungs, lips, and tongues, and doing so in order to request that the other person, across the table there, would be pleased to pass the mashed potatoes. The media involved is largely invisible to us, but it is no less *there* for all that.

In between us and other persons we find a lot of other stuff as well. And over the centuries, we have cooperated together with countless others in order to configure that stuff into large-scale media. We have arranged things so that we can get the word across the planet, or so that we can get something from New Zealand into our inbox in Idaho. Think about what makes up media, including all the aspects of it that we don't tend to notice, as parts of a very complex infra-structure. A list of these things would include your sidewalk, your iPhone, your nearest frontage road, your coat hanger in-side the doorway, your shoes, your car, the calendar hanging in your kitchen, the timer on your coffee pot, the strip where the big box stores are located, and your gas furnace.

When you do something as simple as flipping on a light switch in the morning or programing your coffee pot, you are relying on and interacting with hydroelectric dams, power plants, the fuse box in your mechanical room, the wiring in your house, and the bag of beans you bought from the roaster yesterday. If you touch any part of this invisible spidery web, the whole thing quivers, and in principle, sensitive equipment on the other side of the world could detect that you were up to something.

The theological aspect is found in the reflection that all of this appears to be a design feature. Such things do not get in the way of our essential, interconnected humanness, but rather *express* our essential, interconnected humanness.

When it was just Adam, Eve, Cain, and Abel, they did not need the Internet. Nor could they have built one if they did need it. Neither did they require Interstate highways. And so, some idyllic dreamers have assumed that the ideal condition of man must be the primitive one. But why would we assume that we have lost something essentially human just because we have gotten to the point where there are nearly eight billion of us, and we *do* need an Interstate?

God was the one who told us to multiply. And one of the things that necessarily grows and develops with that multiplication is the largely invisible world of media. When we notice it, which happens rarely, our reflex action is to worry about it—as though getting your news off a smartphone is somehow less "authentic" than getting it from newsprint, telegraphs, or smoke signals.

The reason it is helpful to think in terms of "media," as opposed to the earlier concept of "tools," is that this expansive category helps us see how inescapable it all is. When I say "tools," it is easy to imagine something like a nail gun, and then to reflect on the fact that nail guns are not essential to human flourishing. We got along without them for a long time.

This contributes to the problem that many Christians have, which is assuming that tools are extraneous to our humanity, and not essential. Somebody thought them up, and perhaps they shouldn't have. But when we see that tools are a subset of media, and that media were obviously a gift from God, given to us through the mere fact of creation, we should become much more comfortable with the idea of tools as essential to our humanity.

I mean, I think it is plain that God intended for us to eat the meat of the coconut, which means getting the coconut cracked open. I could drop one from a cliff onto the rocks below, and then go down and get my dinner. That is to apply a coconut to a rock, and involves no tool—just media. But suppose I wanted to simplify my life, and found a rock that

37

fits my hand, and I applied it to the coconut. That is a rudimentary *tool*, one which is no different in principle than the cliff drop. It is simply rock to coconut instead of coconut to rock. But then suppose I shaped the rock artificially so that it is now a stone axe—you see where I am going. Civilization is already on the horizon. Actually, in principle, civilization has already arrived.

So, a right recognition of the inescapability of media helps us to understand that when a man buys a tool belt and fills it up, he is doing something that in principle pleases God. This is what he was created to do.

CHAPTER FIVE

A THEOLOGY OF
MISSIONS AND MEDIA

At the end of the gospel of Mark, Jesus gives His disciples their marching orders. This is not the Great Commission, but it is on the same theme as that commission. Go into *all the world*. When you go into all the world, you will find creatures there. When you find creatures there, you are to proclaim the gospel to every creature.

"And he said unto them, Go ye into all the world, and preach the gospel to every creature" (Mk. 16:15).[1]

My focus here is to address what is meant by "world." And how do we "go into" all the world? Where is it? The short answer is that the world is where the people are. As soon as we are talking about the world, we are talking about other

---

1. There is not space to go into all the reasons for it here, but my argument assumes the canonicity of the last twelve verses of Mark. This is all of piece with my preference for the *textus receptus*. If anyone wants to pursue this, I have laid out some of my reasons in *Mother Kirk* (Moscow, ID: Canon Press, 2001), 51-60.

people, and this brings up the issue of tools of communication, or *media* in the standard use of that term.

When Jesus spoke these words, going into the world meant what we would call *travel* (going from one place to another yourself), and it meant *communication across distance* (going from one place to another by means of media). Communications media at the time largely meant letters, or epistles. We still have *the same basic options*—travel and communications media. The passage of time has *not* changed the options, but has rather simply changed the ease and speed of those options. We *travel* with much greater ease, and we *communicate* with people on the other side of the world with much greater ease. But we are still working with these two basic options.

Let us simply compare biblical times with modern times. Now, as before, there are people who use both options wisely. But now, as then, there are people who talk big, but do little else. Then as now, there were bookworms and basement dudes, hiding from the world through lofty sounding books, posts, tweets, or whatnot, and all because they were scared of girls. As Solomon once put it, there is nothing new under the sun.

So what should we bring with us when we travel? What should we send with our messages when we write? The answer is *Jesus*, but this must be understood rightly. This does not mean that all your Facebook posts have be pictures of saints with three haloes, or that your website has to play Gregorian chant in the background.

The fact is that mankind is created as a tool-making creature. The fact that we have greatly accelerated the pace of these two functions (travel over distance and communication across distance) is nothing new in principle. When Adam made the first axe, was he giving way to a temptation when he decided to try to make it sharper? If you are traveling, you want to get there sooner. If you post a letter, you want it to arrive more rapidly. Who cannot see that figuring out how to do this would constitute improvements? But of course, the improvements will bring a new set of temptations with them, just as the initial invention did.

As argued earlier, Adam was created naked, but given the magnitude of the task he was given—which included digging mines, sailing oceans, and climbing mountains—the creation of tools was an absolute necessity. This means that when *we* make tools, whether plows and shovels, smoke signals or iPhones, we are not violating our essential humanity. Rather we are *expressing* it.

Contrary to the theory of evolution, we are not over-developed animals who moved away from the "natural" and down into the "artificial." For man, the artificial *is* natural. We want nothing to do with Rousseau's "noble savage." Ten minutes after Adam figured out what that honeycomb was, he started looking around for that stick we mentioned earlier.

Now wherever Christians go, they go as themselves.

"Now they which were scattered abroad upon the persecution that arose about Stephen travelled as far as Phenice, and Cyprus, and Antioch, preaching the word . . ." (Acts 11:19a).

Wherever hypocrites go, they also go as themselves.

"Woe unto you, scribes and Pharisees, hypocrites! for ye compass sea and land to make one proselyte, and when he is made, ye make him twofold more the child of hell than yourselves" (Matt. 23:15).

Your country can only export whatever it is your farmers are growing. When you go somewhere, or when you send a message somewhere, you are simply projecting *what you already are*. If you are a bore and a bellygod, then social media will in fact enable you to engage in some digital scribbling so that people in South America can, if they *wish*, read about your grumbles over lunch.

But if you are alive, vibrant, and forgiven, you now live in a world where you can project *that* in amazing ways. The gospel is not some tiresome thing that door-to-door salesmen try to talk you into. "Repent ye therefore, and be converted, that your sins may be blotted out, when *the times of refreshing* shall come from *the presence of the Lord*" (Acts 3:19). We are actually talking about a cool breeze that blows off the ocean of God's infinite pleasure and delight. We are talking about times of *refreshing*, and if we are not talking about times of refreshing, then we are not talking about the gospel as presented in Scripture.

A right understanding of the gospel is therefore delighted, and delightful. Godliness is free in its enjoyment of the pleasures of God. Obedience is liberty. "Whether therefore ye eat, or drink, or whatsoever ye do, do all to the glory of God" (1 Cor. 10:31). This is quite true—whatever you eat or drink, on whatever day, for whatever meal. This includes, of course, the french fries, but that does not mean that you are to stand on the restaurant chair in order to thank God that you are not like other men, the ones who do *not* glorify God for the french fries.

The grace of God is *good*. Do not be like that nun that Brother Lawrence referred to, the one who wanted to be "faster than grace."[2] This is how we run headlong into scruples and fussing and various kinds of wowserism. Enjoy your life, the one Christ has given you. And it is not possible to do this without enjoying Christ Himself.

There is more than one meaning for the word *share*. The charge against the early disciples was that they had "filled Jerusalem" with their teaching, "Saying, Did not we straitly command you that ye should not teach in this name? and, behold, ye have filled Jerusalem with your doctrine, and intend to bring this man's blood upon us" (Acts 5:28).

We do not have pastors and evangelists as hired guns to do all the evangelism for us. They are trained and equipped so that they can prepare God's people for works of service (Eph. 4:12). The saints are to do the work of ministry, although not at the same level as someone gifted or trained. But all of us are involved and engaged. And to be honest, how much training does it take to share or retweet something?

It is not a matter of this technique or that one, this social media trick or that one, but rather experiencing the presence of Christ in your life and communicating *that*. Who is the Lord Jesus? Who is this King of glory? He is, among many other things, the Lord of the Internet. His lordship and His offered forgiveness should therefore be proclaimed there. Why would it not be? Is the world there? Do unforgiven men and women spend a lot of time there?

So, again, what is media? I said earlier that media includes our clothes, other people, tools (especially tools for communication), and infrastructure. These are all means through which Christians communicate—first with God, then with

---

2. Brother Lawrence, *The Practice of the Presence of God* (1693).

the other saints, and then with unbelievers. Respectively, we pray through Christ, we have fellowship in Christ, and we proclaim Christ. What do we use as we do all these things? We use, among other things, ink, newsprint, microphones, email, toner, power point, algorithms, video clips, all of which are made out of *molecules*. They are things.

This means that, because of the way we are created, we cannot love others without media because love, like sound, doesn't travel in a vacuum.

CHAPTER SIX

A THEOLOGY OF MARKETS

I don't get many opportunities for this, so let me take them when I can. I refer, of course, to the exhilarating sensation of disagreeing with C.S. Lewis.

In an essay on good work, Lewis says this:

"For the wearer, zip fasteners have this advantage over buttons: that, while they last, they will save him an infinitesimal amount of time and trouble. For the producer, they have a much more solid merit; they don't remain in working order long. Bad work is the desideratum."

That's it. I disagree with Lewis about zippers.

Well, actually it is about more than that, but hold on a sec. In the same essay, he says this:

"The only hopeful sign at the moment is the 'space race' between America and Russia. Since we have got ourselves into a state where the main problem is not to provide people with what they need or like, but to keep people making

45

things (it hardly matters what), great powers could not easily be better employed but in fabricating costly objects which they then fling overboard. It keeps money circulating and factories working, and it won't do space much harm—or not for a long time."

In sum, Lewis believed that technological innovations were either a trick to get you subsidizing the methods of planned obsolescence, or they were a big waste of money and time.

The actual subject before us is economics, and two other foundational issues related to economics. The first is what happens over time when market choices are left free and untrammeled. The second is the dividends that sheer curiosity pays.

Manufacturers make zippers and try to sell them to diehard button users. Diehard button users can refuse to budge and thereby put the zipper guy out of business, or they can go along. If they go along with the new technology, a certain amount of beta testing is going to occur, and things should improve over time. In other words, as the years go by, you should expect zippers to jam far less than they did in the 1950's. I remember as a kid having far more zipper trouble than I do now. In both cases, the end result is that your pants stay up, and the time involved in getting them on differs only by seconds. So maybe that is not exactly a high-stakes game.

But what about space exploration? God has made the entire universe *fertile*. What looked initially as simply throwing hunks of metal overboard has completely transformed our lives. Because numerous satellites are up there now, I can, with a few clicks of a button on a remote, order a video of Shakespeare or Gilbert & Sullivan on demand in my study. Now it is quite true that somebody else can watch mind-rot dramedies on demand also—but there is nothing new about that. Right? There has never been a time when Simple Simon *couldn't* go to the fair.

Also—because of those satellites—I can take my phone out of my pocket in a strange city, have it tell me where I am within a few feet, and tell me the location of the diner I am looking for. Then I can call the friend who is waiting for me at that diner and tell him I am running late. Then I can look up a book in a library on the other side of the world while I am walking to the diner in order that we might have something to talk about.

We have already considered how wealth is a good thing. We have seen how tools are a particular kind of wealth, and that they are also good. Not only are they good, they are essential to our humanity. These tools are nested within another form of wealth, the blessings of media.

With these assumptions running in the background, we must remember—as we are messing about with our tools— that we cannot plan everything out beforehand. We have to trust God for the future, *always*. If we try to control the future because it makes us nervous, we will only succeed in achieving the disasters we fear. And what we call controlling the future is actually controlling *people*—a point Lewis himself trenchantly makes in *Abolition of Man*—and thereby ruining their lives. He argues in that book that what we call control over nature is actually control over people, with nature as the instrument. We can say the same thing about the future. Control of the future is actually a (vain) attempt to control people, with the future as our instrument.

Two words that do not go together are *control* and *future*. The future, like salvation, is the gift of God, and it must be apprehended by faith alone.

Grinding poverty can certainly come about through natural disasters—famines and so on—but the thing we really need to be on guard against is organized and coercive poverty, by which I mean socialism. Socialism is the drive to control the free choices of other people, especially in the future, in order to prevent them from doing things that seem stupid to the self-appointed organizers, but which will lead to staggering wealth, or so the organizers say, three generations from now.

I do not say this because Lewis was a socialist—he was far, far from it—but I do want to maintain that there are times when conservative curmudgeons can play into the hands of these poverty organizers.

The two issues mentioned earlier that underlie economics are first, the need for us to respect the free choices of others, and second, to use our own power of free choice to investigate the fruitful world God gave to us. We leave the results (the future) to God. A national economy on any given day is the sum total of all the economic decisions that are made by all the individuals in that country throughout the course of the day. And this all relates to our productivity and the work we are assigned to do.

If we resist the temptation to meddle, if we let the free market just run, we will find that the zippers improve over time. They had better. And this is not a form of idolatry called "trusting the free market," or some abstraction called "capitalism." To speak about markets, or Adam Smith's invisible hand, is to use a form of shorthand. When we speak about the law of supply and demand (outside the control of any human agency), we are talking about the Author of that law, and of others. (I refer to the law of gravity, for example, or the three laws of motion.) In other words, the free market does not decide the price of the new zippers. That decision is made by the Lord Jesus.

A statement like that hits us sideways because we are accustomed to think about the world in quasi-Deistic terms. Sure, God made everything some time long ago, but things happen now because of impersonal natural laws, right? Gravity pulls things to the floor, centrifugal force pulls them out to the edges, and the law of supply and demand determines the cost of zippers. But the biblical doctrine is actually one of creation and ongoing providence. All of it is personal.

We demonstrate that we understand this by expressing our gratitude for God's past goodness to us and by trusting Him for His future goodness. As I said, one necessary aspect of that trust is the refusal to try to *control* the future through utopian schemes. God will provide.

When we refrain from trying to run the economic choices or ventures being made by others, we are opening ourselves up for dislocations. So trusting Him in this takes diligence. Sometimes it looks as though we have to step in. Dislocations might be mild, as happened with the button industry, or they might be huge, as we saw in the Industrial Revolution, and now again in the Digital Revolution.

Whether we are talking about a small-scale disruption or a large one, there is one sure thing about it. If slipshod work is allowed to fail, then quality work will remain. The external pressures of the free market with ensure that. But for

Christians who want to be faithful in their work, their internal motivation will also contribute to the quality of the work.

We are to put our hand to the work, doing the best we can with it, and we are to keep our hands *off* the future.

"Do you see a man skillful in his work? He will stand before kings; he will not stand before obscure men" (Prov. 22:29, ESV).

Notice how this works. What happens in the future—the standing before kings part—is in the hands of God. My work is in the hands of God also, but in a different sense (Eph. 2:10). So my responsibility is, so to speak, whatever is in front of me, there on my workbench or desk or counter. I should do a first-rate job with *that*, and other things will fall into place. And as they fall into place, it will not be the impersonal doing of Adam Smith's invisible hand.

Every blessing a Christian ever receives is from a pierced hand.

CHAPTER SEVEN

A THEOLOGY
OF PROGRESS

Putting this all together, we need to come back to our theology of wealth for a moment.

Remember, wealth is a blessing, and what you do with it matters. What you do with wealth will either keep it a compounding blessing, or it will wreck everything. But when it is first poured out on you, it is a blessing.

So now we need to talk about another particular kind of wealth—the wealth composed of technological progress over time.

Wealth is a function of accumulated man hours. And in another way, wealth is the ability to command the labor of another—the ability to tap into some portion of those available man hours. This accumulation of man hours can come in one of two forms, or in a combination of the two. The first is a large enough population size to allow any specialist to be summoned, and the second is the incarnation of a specialist's knowledge in a tool.

If one hundred moderns were gathered up and deposited on an uninhabited tropical island and left there for five hundred years, what would happen? Let us assume that their number included mechanical engineers, accountants, carpenters, software engineers, copy machine repairmen, plumbers, and so on. The works. This does not change or alter the fact that for the first twenty years or so they are all going to be hustling for coconuts. Once they have the survival question more or less settled, they can then spend their twilight years sitting around campfires, telling their children and grandchildren stories about the "old times."

These stories would be about 747s, smartphones, cable television, antibiotics, x-ray machines, and so on. And the attitude of the grandchildren would range from credulous amazement to skeptical disbelief—because even though the storytellers might know how such things are built, they would not have the available man hours to build any of them.

They would not even have the available man hours to build a No. 2 pencil. They would need the metal that holds the eraser, and that means mining and smelting. They would need the synthetic rubber for the eraser, and a manufacturing plant to make it. And the yellow paint—they need some place that makes the yellow paint. And somebody has to mine and process the graphite. In short, in order to make a No. 2 pencil, we need hundreds of thousands of man hours that these people on the island don't have. We have former engineers who have gotten good at gathering coconuts. That, and telling wild stories to their grandkids.

This is how someone like da Vinci could invent a bunch of things that he couldn't build—helicopters, parachutes, machine guns, etc. He did not have the available man hours that a modern economy provides—and a modern economy is dependent upon a large population size. He had the smarts, but he didn't have the wealth. He could not summon the labor of others. It was not there to be summoned. It did not exist.

The Industrial Revolution put those man hours on the ground, in factories, near big cities. The Digital Revolution has taken those man hours, multiplied them greatly, and put them all in your pocket. After the Industrial Revolution, a man who wanted milled textiles could put an order in to a factory in Manchester, England, and the fabric would be shipped to him some weeks later. He had "servants" over there, and he could summon their labor. They were "time share" servants, but he had wealth (as we are discussing it in this chapter) in that he could command the labor of others. When he did so, the effects were disproportionately large—as compared to what would have happened if Nebuchadnezzar in his day had ordered the same number of yards of cloth. Our modern man got what he ordered a lot faster and a lot cheaper than Nebuchadnezzar would have. That fabled king of Babylon would have needed to issue a command to thousands of weavers.

However, there is a hitch. Wealth is the technical ability to summon the labor of others, either in person or through the application of tools, but the person in possession of that wealth has to have the ability to know how to do it. I hope that you see that our definition of wealth hasn't *changed*, but it is certainly getting more texture. Imagine a person of modest means who wins some kind of intergalactic lottery, and inherits a mansion the size of Rhode Island, staffed with 10,000 servants. Things are not going to run well *automatically*. His new wealth must be managed. Servants must be supervised. Workers must be given direction. In other words, wealth brings a great deal of responsibility to the wealthy.

If this newly wealthy person does not rise to the occasion, the end of the story will be 9,000 servants sitting on the back veranda, smoking cigarettes and passing the time.

Now, if you have a smartphone in your pocket, one of the things you also have in your pocket is 9,000 servants sitting on the veranda. Lest you think I am overstating it, try a small thought experiment. Julius Caesar and George Washington got around their respective worlds in basically the same way. Transportation was either horse drawn or sail driven for both men. That being the case, let us pick on George Washington. What would he have needed to have there at Mount Vernon in order to be able even to approximate what you have the ability to order up (with your *thumb*) on the phone in your pocket?

He would have needed at *least* 10,000 servants. Let me use the example of just a few of the apps that are sitting there on my phone right this minute. I have a program to tutor me in French. I have a guitar tuner. I have a church directory. I have a calculator. I have someone to read me books in a British accent. I have access to libraries all around the world. I have a camera. And on and on and on.

And to be honest, I have a handful of reliable servants that I go to again and again. But most of my servants, well over 9,000, are sitting around on their butts. And even the programs that

I do use are operating at about 5% of their capacity. In short, I am not nearly as good a boss as I ought to be.

In other words, if you are anything like me, you need to learn how to manage this embarrassment of wealth. In short, you need to learn how to become more productive. Put another way, you need to read the second section of this book.

It is almost time to lean into the progress. But one more warning first.

CHAPTER EIGHT

A THEOLOGY OF GLAD SUSPICION

If we were to look up "technology" in a concordance, we would find that the Bible teaches us almost nothing about it. If we were to look up the idea of "progress," we wouldn't find anything on that either. So let us emphasize this yet again: Technology is a form of wealth; progress is a form of wealth. This helps us get our bearings as Christians, because we should now know what to watch out for.

If these are forms of wealth, then we know that they are good things, blessings from God, and we also know that they are very dangerous things. The Bible does teach us what our orientation toward wealth should be—that of glad suspicion, or maybe, on our gloomy days, suspicious gladness.

God blesses nations with wealth, and in the same breath He tell us to watch our step. Here are those ten verses from Deuteronomy again:

When thou hast eaten and art full, then thou shalt bless the Lord thy God for the good land which he hath given thee. Beware that thou forget not the Lord thy God, in not keeping his commandments, and his judgments, and his statutes, which I command thee this day: Lest when thou hast eaten and art full, and hast built goodly houses, and dwelt therein; And when thy herds and thy flocks multiply, and thy silver and thy gold is multiplied, and all that thou hast is multiplied; Then thine heart be lifted up, and thou forget the Lord thy God, which brought thee forth out of the land of Egypt, from the house of bondage; Who led thee through that great and terrible wilderness, wherein were fiery serpents, and scorpions, and drought, where there was no water; who brought thee forth water out of the rock of flint; Who fed thee in the wilderness with manna, which thy fathers knew not, that he might humble thee, and that he might prove thee, to do thee good at thy latter end; And thou say in thine heart, My power and the might of mine hand hath gotten me this wealth. But thou shalt remember the Lord thy God: for it is he that giveth thee power to get wealth, that he may establish his covenant which he sware unto thy fathers, as it is this day. And it shall be, if thou do at all forget the Lord thy God, and walk after other gods, and serve them, and worship them, I testify against you this day that ye shall surely perish. As the nations which the Lord destroyeth before your face, so shall ye perish; because ye would not be obedient unto the voice of the Lord your God. (Deut. 8:10-20)

There it is, all in a nutshell. God gives us the wealth that we will be tempted to put in place of Him. When God does this, we may show ourselves ingrates by turning away from Him, wealth in hand, or by throwing the wealth to the ground in front of Him. The technophile just assumes that man is the measure of all things, and he plumps his resume in order to get a job with Google, so that he too may become one of the lords of the earth. The technophobe just memorizes the poetry of Wendell Berry, and yearns for the days of yesterday when all our food was eked out under a hot sun by a slow mule and a picturesque peasant staggering behind it. Both are forms of ingratitude; both are grotesque. The only *obedient* response is to accept that wealth as the gift of God that it is, and to keep it in its proper creaturely place.

Because it is a form of wealth, the bias contained within technological advancements is toward forgetting God. Because it is a form of wealth, cultural progress does veer toward disobedience. Jeshurun waxes fat and kicks. What else is new?

Although there is a bias toward sin in the possession of such blessings, it is important to emphasize by means of reiteration that sin is not resident within the things themselves. In this respect, it is like the old covenant—God finds fault with the *people* (Heb. 8:7-8). There is no sin in immunizations, in iPhones, in Google searches, in air travel, or in Lasik eye surgery. To the extent it is progress, it is the result of God's kindness as mediated through our culture as fruit of the gospel.

Earlier in this book, I dismissed those who would love to get a brain drive that would enable them to speak Spanish fluently, and I applauded those who modify their God-given condition as they do things like getting braces for their kids' teeth, as they mow the lawn, and even as they comb their hair. But where is the line between godly dominion and godless interference? How would we identify sin?

Let us break this question into two pieces, giving a paragraph to each one. There are many lawful things to do as we exercise dominion in the world, but which can be done with a sinful motive. You mow your lawn, but it is because you are in a hot envy competition with your neighbor and *his* lawn. You get braces for your daughter's teeth because you are hellbent on her becoming Miss America someday. Nothing wrong with the mower or the braces, but a lot wrong with what is going on down in the heart. This problem of motive is addressed through simple repentance.

But there is another category of technological development—say, longing for the day when genetic engineers can splice the genes of a silverback gorilla into a developing human fetus, in search of the ultimate NFL linebacker. Such things are *malum in se*, wrong in themselves. And they are wrong in themselves because the people engaged in such activities are seeking *to play God*. They are overtly rejecting the fact of a Creator God, the words of Scripture, and the authority of natural law. What they are doing is wicked. They want to tinker with man according to their own whims, which is to say, they want to be able to make man in *their* image. And that is the problem. The problem is not mere fact of a *tool* like genetic engineering. If genetic engineers at some point enable us to cure Down's syndrome, we should thank God, and it is no more problematic than a doctor setting a broken bone. This is merely submitting to the pattern for humanity given to us by a gracious God. We can readily identify that pattern even though it has been marred by the fact of a fallen world. This is radically different from those who want to make up their own world.

We cannot examine the rise of technological blessings without focusing on those nations where the gospel took deepest root. If we couple this with an understanding that the gospel fulfills the promises given in the Old Testament (instead of abrogating them), this would of necessity include the blessings promised in Deuteronomy. What is happening should not astonish us. It is our promised legacy.

To whatever extent it is not a blessing, it is not progress. If it is progress, then we must thank God for it—He is the one who gives us the power to get wealth, and there is no appropriate or safe response to that wealth other than complete and simple gratitude.

At the same time, we must recognize that things are muddled up even further by those people who call themselves progressives, who have absolutely no standard to measure progress by, and hence no way of defining whether or not progress has occurred. They like it this way because shortly after their policies kick in, everything starts to look pretty regressive. But they can't see that because they insist on standing backwards, facing up the down escalator.

Now, Americans are bottom line people, and we like to check how the Dow is doing, and what the GDP has been up to lately. And so here is the takeaway cash value to this particular point: *In the long run, pragmatism doesn't work*. Focusing on the GDP alone is bad for the GDP. It does not profit a man to gain the world and lose his soul, and there is an additional sting when he then loses the world too. Whatever you worship in place of God is another thing you lose. Whatever you surrender gladly to Him is returned to you, pressed down, shaken, and running over.

There is not one blessing that we enjoy that was not given to us by the hand of Jesus Christ. If we insist on ignoring His lordship, His blood, His authority, and His kindness, then the time is coming, and now is, when He will chastise us by taking it all away. If we seek first the Kingdom, then other things will be added. If we don't acknowledge Him, worship Him, or bow down before Him, He takes away that which was blocking the view, which in our case is all our *stuff.*

In a number of other places, I have repeatedly argued for a new Christendom, a mere Christendom, and this is the financial argument for it. We cannot have the blessings of God if we hate the God who alone can give these blessings. This is not merchandising the gospel. Let us not teeter along on the rim of some health and wealth nonsense, but at the same time, let us give the steely eye of rebuke to those Christian leftists who want to dance along the other rim of disease and poverty, once those progressive ideals have been suitably renamed.

We need to learn how to be motivated by the things which God uses to motivate us. Among other reasons, the prodigal son returned home in true repentance *because he was famished* (Lk. 15:17). His stomach was part of the reason for his repentance (Prov. 16:26).

But shouldn't we repent for the purest of motives? Doesn't work that way. If we had pure motives, we wouldn't be needing to repent. When God establishes the nations of the next Christendom, He considers our frame. He takes us by the hand and teaches us that He is not mocked—a man reaps what he sows, and so do nations. If we do it God's way, we live in His favor. If we refuse to live God's way, we suffer the consequences. If we go this way, good things happen, and if we go that way, bad things happen. And to keep us from getting confused, God gave us a book explaining all of that.

Some might object, thinking that this is just simplistic in the extreme. They want a more sophisticated religion than that—for a sophisticated, industrialized, advanced nation. Well, just between us girls, I am not sure we are all that sophisticated. For example, to stay with the subject of wealth and poverty, if the Pacific Ocean were red ink, we are currently hunched over in a bathysphere, deep within trillions of gallons of it, down in the Mariana Trench somewhere. And it was our *smart* guys who decided to do that, you know?

So once we have the attitude of glad suspicion down, we can move on to the nuts and bolts—whether spiritual or practical.

PART TWO

LEARNING
PLODUCTIVITY

AN INTRODUCTION
TO PLODUCTIVITY

The first step toward genuinely productive work is to make it a point to work *coram Deo*, in the presence of God. I don't mean to limit this to formalities like opening with prayer or closing with a benediction, but this certainly means *more* than just some kind of formal recognition. And by saying this I don't mean to imply that opening and closing with prayer is necessarily a "formality." No, not at all. But if it is limited to that, it soon will be a dead formality.

In Scripture we are told to pray without ceasing (1 Thess. 5:17). We are told that whatever we do, down to the eating and drinking, we are to do it to the glory of God (1 Cor. 10:31). And we are told to present our bodies as living sacrifices to God, holy and acceptable (Rom. 12:1-2).

Now if my body is a living sacrifice, this means that everything it rests upon is an altar. The car I drive is an altar, the bed I sleep in is an altar, and the desk where I work is an *altar*.

Everything is offered to God, everything ascends to Him as a sweet-smelling savor. Faith is the fire of the altar, and it consumes the whole burnt offering, the ascension offering. What ascends to the Lord is the sweet savor of our good works: "So as to walk in a manner worthy of the Lord, fully pleasing to him: bearing fruit in every good work and increasing in the knowledge of God" (Col. 1:10, ESV). Bearing fruit in every good work is *fully pleasing to Him.*

The works that ascend before Him are the works that He prepared beforehand for us to do. He gives us the works that are intended to return to Him. "For we are his workmanship, created in Christ Jesus unto good works, which God hath before ordained that we should walk in them" (Eph. 2:10). Those works include, but are not limited to, writing code, making birdhouses, repairing a carburetor, outlining a novel, or manufacturing microchips.

Living and working in the presence of God is essential because what constitutes a truly productive person is the fact that they are laboring under the blessing of God. This is because you can have people who strive to do everything technically right, but it is somehow not *blessed*. There are others who look to the world like they are a walking slapdash, and yet everything lands right side up for them. They are blessed. And there are two other categories as well—there are folks who do everything wrong, and it looks like it, as we see with the sluggard in Proverbs, and then you have that irritating handful of people who do everything right, *and* they are blessed by God on top of everything else.

Living in the presence of God means that you are living in such a way as to invite or seek His favor. The Sabbath and the tithe illustrate well the trust we are to display in this. Would you rather work hard for seven unblessed days, or work hard for six blessed days? Would you rather try to live on 100% of an unblessed income or on 90% of a blessed income? Would you rather have smaller barns blessed or larger barns unblessed (Lk. 12:20)? "Except the LORD build the house, they labour in vain that build it: Except the LORD keep the city, the watchman waketh but in vain" (Ps. 127:1).

As we look for the blessing of God, we need to be mindful of what kind of blessing we are looking for. What I am talking about is Deuteronomic blessings, the kind of blessing that increases both your basket and your store (Deut. 28:5). I am talking about the kind of blessing that lands on your productivity. "And let the beauty of the LORD our God be upon us: And establish thou the work of our hands upon us; Yea, *the work of our hands* establish thou it" (Ps. 90:17).

Pray that God establish the work of your *hands*, and not just the work of your heart. This is not a facile "health and wealth" approach because God is not to be treated as some kind of a vending machine. God's blessing includes both temporal victories and temporal defeats, and evangelical faith knows how to handle all of it. Some subdued kingdoms and received their dead back to life again, while others were flogged and imprisoned (Heb. 11:33-39). Some lived in palaces and some in caves, but faithfulness knows how to live in either place. At the same time, although the faith can thrive in times of persecution, we are not to pray for persecution. We are instructed to pray for quiet and peaceable lives (1 Tim. 2:2). A Christian should be able to be content whether he is out in the cold, or inside by the fire (Phil. 4:12). But even so, everything else being equal, the apostle Paul knew enough to come in out of the rain. We know which way to go, which way to pray, which direction to set our sights as we work.

So with hunger for God's blessing as the foundation of our settled demeanor and attitude, we may now turn to some more practical considerations. We will still be doing theology, but we are going to be doing it now in the office, the study, the workshop, and the kitchen.

CHAPTER NINE

THE FINITUDE
OF WORK

Regarding the principle that the hippies taught us so many years ago, which is that we should bloom where we are planted, next let's consider some aspects of this that might affect our work.

If we begin the work rightly, then we will be looking at our future productivity in a much more biblical way. Beginning where we are, let us consider the pressing reality that our work is finite. This is because it is the work that we are assigned to do, and *we* are finite. In the cosmic scheme of things, the work that is assigned to us, and which God has given us to do, is *tiny*. The work that we will do by the grace of God, and to which God will respond with "well done, good and faithful servant," will be work that is teeny tiny. Finitude is one of our *glories*. God will not say *well done* to any human whose work is the size of three galaxies. He will say *well done* to pipsqueaks with a couple of fists full of nanoworks. We sometimes marvel at those dedicated engravers who can carve the Lord's Prayer on the head of a pin, but we must always remember that our Creator put our whole *planet* on the head of a pin. A short space of time looking through a telescope should convince you that we actually live in Whoville.

Too many people confound our finitude with our sinfulness, but the breach between us and God is one that was caused by our unholiness, not by our size. Before Adam sinned he was just as small as the day after he sinned, but he was still able to walk with God in the garden in the cool of the day. Our size is a feature, not a bug.

Now if we were placed in this world in order to work before the Lord, and if the Lord ordained good works beforehand for us to do, and if He intended us to do *good* by those good works, this means that we do not have to have the big picture in order to work productively and faithfully. This is good because we are too small to have the big picture.

We are God's workmanship, created in Christ Jesus to do good works, which God prepared beforehand for us to do. God is up to something big—He has a cosmic project in view—and not one of us knows the fullness of what that is. "But as it is written, Eye hath not seen, nor ear heard, neither have entered into the heart of man, the things which God hath prepared for them that love him" (1 Cor. 2:9). At the same time, this "thing we know not what" is something that all of us are going to help bring about. God designs the huge projects and He assigns all the bit parts to all the little people. He says to Smith that he is to stand in this particular spot, and when the whistle blows, he is to pull that lever. *Why?* Smith wonders. *Just pull the lever,* God replies.

God is not being coy with us. We don't have the capacity yet to understand the majestic sweep of what He is up to. An essential part of the way that we will *gain* that capacity over time is by being faithful in the little parts we are given to do first. He who is faithful over little will be faithful over much (Lk. 19:17). And I would venture to add that he who is faithful over little will come to understand more and much more.

George MacDonald once said that obedience is the great opener of eyes. The more we do, the more we will be able to do. The more we learn, the more we know, and one of the things we know is how to learn more. But in order to get the requisite experience, we have to be content with our limited range for a while. For a little bit, battling impatience, we learn how to pull the lever, and how to fight off temptations to go off to do something else. That something else is, in our imagination, a very important thing, and it has an imagined importance that makes sense to us. It is a creature of ours. And if it makes complete sense to us, then it is a sure thing that we are flying blinkered and blind. As Thomas Chalmers put it, "Regardless of how large, your vision is too small." The only way our work can be large enough is if it is submitted entirely to the will of God—and we demonstrate our understanding of that by staying at our post and pulling the lever when the whistle blows.

We discussed the problem of the desert-island No. 2 pencil earlier. In a famous 1958 essay, *I Pencil*, Leonard Read showed that no man on earth knows how to make a pencil. No one man can accomplish all the things that need to be accomplished for this to happen, but pencils are manufactured anyway, and they are made because hundreds of men do the things, things near to them, that they *can* do. They all do things that are within their reach. But not one of them can make a pencil.

When God created *ex nihilo*, He was doing *all* the work. When we work as sub-creators, to use Tolkien's word for it, we are dealing with pre-existent materials and processes. This is because God is using the miniscule works that we are performing to teach us to trust Him, and to teach us the meaning of work. But the meaning of that work is not that we are doing all of it, or even a significant portion of it. Take a talented gardener, for example, with a greenhouse full of exquisite orchids. He gets up early and works late. He studies his vocation and loves it in an ordinate way. We would say he grows beautiful flowers, but when we step back and think about it, out of all the work that is being done in that greenhouse, what percentage of it is the gardener doing? One percent? And what percentage is God doing in and through that mysterious instrument of His called *life*?

"I have planted, Apollos watered; but God gave the increase. So then neither is he that planteth any thing, neither he that watereth; but God that giveth the increase" (1 Cor. 3:6–7).

Remembering the finitude of your labors will keep you humble. Recognizing that your labors have a place in God's cosmic intentions for the universe will keep you from thinking that your tiny labors are stupid labors. They are nothing of the kind. Your labors in the Lord are not in vain (1 Cor. 15:58).

CHAPTER TEN

AMBITION IS
A GOOD THING

If we learn the lessons from the previous chapter, we will understand that our works are small, just as we are small. They do not have an absolute importance, however vain we might be about them. At the same time, there is nothing wrong with us wanting the work we do to be significant, as measured on a human scale. And this is where godly ambition comes in.

Our ambitions for our work should be comparatively large, but they ought not to be cosmic. If we are plowing a small field, we should certainly want to learn how to plow one that is just a little bigger. We should want to figure out how to get more bushels per acre out of that field. Sure. But this is quite different than wanting to ascend to the sides of the north, to sit on the mount of the congregation.

Of course there is such a thing as ungodly ambition, and it is truly destructive. "For where jealousy and selfish ambition exist, there will be disorder and every vile practice" (Jas. 3:16, ESV). And the Lord Jesus established the pattern for us, the pattern of turning away from every form of vainglory. "And I seek not mine own glory . . ." (Jn. 8:50). But we are *not* to combat this kind of grasping ambition with a Buddhist rejection of desire. The true Christian is characterized, not by a *lack* of desire, but rather through a desire that is calibrated to its appropriate object, which is ultimately Christ.

God created us for glory, and there is no way for us to find a switch that will turn that off. We are inveterate glory-seekers, and the thing that distinguishes a good man from a bad man is *what* he finds glorious—not whether he finds something glorious. Scripture even describes sin in terms of falling short of glory. "For all have sinned, and come short of the glory of God" (Rom. 3:23).

It is not a sin to pursue glory. It is not a sin to be ambitious for glory. It is actually a sin to surrender your glory. "They exchanged the glory of God for the image of an ox that eats grass" (Ps. 106:20, ESV)

The pursuit of salvation is described by the apostle Paul as the pursuit of glory. Eternal life is the inheritance of those *who patiently seek glory*, among other things. "To them who by patient continuance in well doing *seek for glory* and honour and immortality, eternal life" (Rom. 2:7). "The wise shall *inherit glory*: But shame shall be the promotion of fools" (Prov. 3:35). "Let the saints be *joyful in glory*: Let them sing aloud upon their beds" (Ps. 149:5).

Many Christians think their problem lies in the verbs, when it actually lies in the direct objects and in the adverbs. They think they are to be faulted because they *want*, because they *desire*. But the actual problem is not that we desire, but that we desire the wrong things, or that we desire the right things wrongly. We are not supposed to love the world, or the things in it (1 Jn. 2:15-16). We are not supposed to ask for good things wrongly, that we may spend them on our desires (Jas. 4:3). But when we discover these disordered sins in our motives, we are not supposed go off to find the spigot that controls our "wanting" and turn it entirely off. That is not the solution at all. We are called, rather, to take the garden hose, with the water running, and go water the petunias with it. We are supposed to stop watering the Canadian thistles, which are chest high already.

"We are half-hearted creatures, fooling about with drink and sex and ambition when infinite joy is offered us, like an ignorant child who wants to go on making mud pies in a slum because he cannot imagine what is meant by the offer of a holiday at the sea. We are far too easily pleased."[3]

Lewis is here speaking of the permanent things, the realms of eternity. This should never be forgotten, but we must also not forget that the principle applies to our lives down here, before we cross over Jordan. And what principle is that? *We are far too easily pleased.* We settle.

And this is where the Spirit must do His miraculous work. He enables forgiven sinners to attempt audacious things, and to do so without vainglory or lust for an ego shrine built in one's own honor.

Now there is nothing wrong with a man settling into his place, the place that God has assigned to him. "For I say,

3. C.S. Lewis, *The Weight of Glory* (Grand Rapids: Eerdmans, 1972), 2.

through the grace given unto me, to every man that is among you, not to think of himself more highly than he ought to think; but to think soberly, according as God hath dealt to every man the measure of faith" (Rom. 12:3). But there *is* something wrong with a man settling too quickly, for the sake of avoiding too much responsibility or too much work. That dreaded comment on our report cards when we were little often had a bit of wisdom in it for us: "Not working up to his potential." If we are doing all we can, if we are maxed out, then of course it is not necessary to do what we simply cannot do. But we should not kid ourselves in this regard. We often have hidden reserves that even we do not suspect.

Setting ambitious goals is therefore a good thing, and determining whether or not we are desiring something sinful, or desiring it sinfully, is heart work. We do that heart work by praying to the Lord about it, by reading the Word faithfully, looking to be instructed, and by worshiping God together with His people, gathering regularly to be edified by Word and sacrament. Every week you place all your ambitions on His altar and watch them ascend to Heaven in a column of smoke. When you get to your office Monday morning, they will be there on your desk, cleansed and waiting for you.

CHAPTER ELEVEN

THE MASTER KEY

The idea of mastery is to develop genuine expertise within the radius or labor that God has given you, such that when you ask God—Jabez-like—to enlarge your border, you can do it with a clean conscience (1 Chron. 4:10). The kind of ambition that wants to clamber over half-finished work in your initial radius of influence, in order to get that next promotion, is an ambition that is being driven by the wrong kind of motivation entirely. Do you see a man who excels in his work? *He* will stand before kings (Prov. 22:29).

Craft competence is a virtue to be cultivated. What were the musicians in Israel called to do? "Sing unto him a new song; *Play skillfully* with a loud noise" (Ps. 33:3).

How was Aaron's ephod to be made? "And they shall make the ephod of gold, of blue, and of purple, of scarlet, and fine twined linen, *with cunning work*" (Exod. 28:6).

What kind of work does the Lord praise, when He compares it to the beauty of the Shulamite? "How beautiful are thy feet with shoes, O prince's daughter! The joints of thy thighs are like jewels, *the work of the hands of a cunning workman*" (Song 7:1).

"Bezalel and Oholiab and every craftsman *in whom the LORD has put skill and intelligence* to know how to do any work in the construction of the sanctuary shall work in accordance with all that the LORD has commanded" (Exod. 36:1, ESV).

It is impossible to read through the Scriptures and come to the conclusion that the Lord thinks slipshod work is good enough. I have mentioned that over the years I have had far too many dealings with Christian merchants, builders, professionals, and so on, who have somehow incorporated into their mission statement something along the lines of "Christians aren't perfect, just forgiven." Again, while it is true that our salvation is by grace through faith, not of works lest any man boast, it remains true that if you routinely install people's cabinets upside down, the word will get around town. And that will have an effect on your business, an effect that is *not* achieved by grace through faith.

So the first step in achieving mastery is *taking responsibility* for the results. You should know what the best practices are. You should constantly be learning something fresh and new in your field. When something blows up, as it will invariably do sometimes in this fallen world, you communicate with your customers and your creditors, refusing to make them chase you. You tell the truth, and you do not resort to those evasive half-truths called excuses.

Mastery is quite different from getting a promotion, which is often the result of mastery—but not always. Some want the results of mastery without all the tedious efforts that go into attaining to mastery. But the goal is not simply to get promoted into fifth grade. The goal is to master the material in fourth grade and deserve the promotion. Learning the material in your classes, learning your vocation, learning your trade, are what we should actually be after. Things like grades, promotions, bonuses, etc. are merely measuring sticks designed to tell us if we have met the goal. They are not the goal itself, but simply indicators of it.

So while it is reasonable to glance at the measuring stick goal from time to time, for the most part our gaze should be fixed on the work that is before us. Work for the work, not the award. Those who work for the work, and not the award, are—get this—more likely to win the award. Good students who are always asking, "Will that be on the test?" are students who will likely not profit long term from their labors.

And some, unfortunately, through a long striving after A's have learned how to work for the award, and they do not understand the concept of an overall mission at all. This means that when you are looking to master your work, that work which is within your reach, you have to realize that within your circle of influence there are two things you can see. You can see the measurements of what you are doing, and you can see what you are actually doing. The point is to look through the measurements at the task itself, and not at the measurements as though *they* were the task itself. To fall into this mistake is simply another way of abandoning the work you were assigned.

Another key to mastery is realizing that the key to originality is imitation. There are two aspects to this imitation. First, if you pick a good model to imitate, this prevents bad things from happening when you apply the third key (which is repetition). Practicing something wrong is only going to help you learn how to do it wrong. If you pick a *good* model—for guitar playing, for changing spark plugs, for baking strudels, for writing software—you are guarding against the plague that afflicts many beginners, which is the plague of shortcuts. When you take guitar lessons, for example, and you sit down with the guitar on your lap, a comment you will likely hear from your instructor repeatedly is, "No, not that way." There is a way that seemeth right unto a man. The way you want to hold your left hand is not the way you ought to be holding your left hand.

The second good thing about imitation is that it enables you to build on the good work that others have done, which is really the only healthy direction that originality can go. A poet who has mastered (by imitation) all the classic forms of poetry might be in a good position to develop a new and challenging form. But if he passes by all that, and sits down to write poetry that just expresses himself, then he is likely only to achieve a form of free verse that was invented by junior-high girls who had just finished sobbing.

Learn what good work is, imitate it studiously, and do that over time. The result will frequently be what others call inspired or original or creative. Lewis again: "No man who values originality will ever be original. But try to tell the truth as you see it, try to do any bit of work as well as it can be done for the work's sake, and what men call originality will come unsought."[4]

The third key to mastery is repetition. This is why piano students practice their scales over and over and over again. They are not trying to learn the *concept*; they want their finger bones to know all by themselves what to do. I took piano lessons for a very brief time as a child, and I still remember the concept of the C scale—thumb, forefinger, middle finger, thumb under, and so on. But knowing that is not the same thing as having the ability to play that scale fluidly. In order to do that, I would have to practice it a couple hundred thousand times.

When people do something over and over again—and this should not come as a surprise—they get good at it. But to some, this seems suspiciously like work.

---

4. C.S. Lewis, "Membership" in *Essay Collection & Other Short Pieces* (London: Harper Collins, 2000), 340.

CHAPTER TWELVE

THE POWER
OF PLODDING

Those who value productivity highly have a tendency to give way to two very powerful temptations and so to overlook the power of plodding. If they feel the urgent call to productivity, they tend to give way to the blind guides of *intensity* or *extension*.

Intensity is manifested when the deadline approaches and the manager of the project gets some lighter fluid, douses his hair with it, sets it ablaze, and runs around in tight little circles. *Extension* is the solution called "working late." Intensity says that forty-eight hours of work needs to be crammed into a 24-hour day. Extension says that work days need to be extended to fourteen hours instead of eight.

Of course, when the ox is in the ditch or the house is in fact on fire, either one of these options is a very reasonable course to take. There are times when there are actual emergencies. Aliens really are landing on your corporation's heliport. If such were to happen, then of course, behave accordingly. Hunker down.

However, when everything is a crisis, nothing is a crisis. When *every* project or deadline is on fire, this is a time management issue. When it is a routine pattern, the crisis is not in the work, but rather in the worker.

What this means is that productive work requires a rhythm, a metronome. Long distance runners settle into a pace. Rowers in crew fall into what they call "swing." This action, performed at this pace, methodically and deliberately, will in fact get us where we are going. When the need is urgent, the temptation to flail must be resisted. When the need is urgent, the temptation to sprawl must be resisted.

Many people put off working on something until they have been able to "carve out" adequate time to work on it. They need elbow room in order to get it done, and since they never get the adequate elbow room, they never get the work done. "I could write the great American novel if I only had three months free and clear . . ." And of course, three free months, free and clear, are not to be had.

But fifteen minutes a day *can* be had. *That* can be found. Here is the power of plodding. Suppose you wanted to write a novel of sixty thousand words. Daunting, right? That's a big steak there. Carve it up into bite-sized pieces. Commit to writing a hundred words a day, no matter what.

After ten days you have a thousand words. After a month you have three thousand. At this rate you have your novel in under two years—twenty months to be exact. This is not actually a secret for writing a novel; it is a secret for writing a novel that nobody had any idea you were writing.

But you likely have another spare fifteen minutes a day lying about, not to mention some other possible projects you have your eye on. Chip away at them. Do a little bit, and do not fall for the idea that unless you can pour yourself into something for half a year, there is no point doing it at all. And if you say that you could not possibly do anything like this without outlining the whole thing first, well, fine. Work on an outline for fifteen minutes a day.

Take another example in reading. Instead of waiting for that week at the beach when you can plow through three potboilers at one go, decide what you want to read, and then read ten pages of that book every evening. If you have more time available, and the inclination, then go ahead a read a bit more. But give yourself time to read ten pages *daily*. That's ten or fifteen minutes for an average reader. After thirty days, that is a three-hundred-page book.

Change the illustration a bit, but keep it a whacking great big book—365 pages, say. You don't have to write a book review or anything, and so there are no deadlines beyond that of simply completing the book. You just think it is high time you read whatever book it is.

Moby Dick it is. If you made a point of reading just one page a day, you would compete the book in a year. An average reader clocks in around 350 words a minute, and that is about how many words are on an average page. One minute a day, and by the time next year's New Year's resolutions roll around, *blam*, you will have finished it.

I say this from experience. What plodding requires is predictability and routine. This is not a process that thrives in the midst of chaos. So if you are one of those rare souls who can live for twenty-eight days running without any one of those days bearing the least resemblance to any of the others, then this advice about plodding will probably be ineffectual. But if you are like most people, you brush your teeth at approximately the same time every day, have your breakfast the same way, go to lunch like that, and go to bed at roughly the same time.

Most of us could answer the question, "What time do you usually go to bed?" Well, my advice is to go to bed fifteen minutes later. And you will discover that if you prioritize getting your fifteen minutes of whatever it is in, you can usually fit it in earlier and keep your bedtime.

This is another way of saying that an awful lot of us waste an awful lot of time. We blow our fifteen-minute opportunities like they grew on trees. This is not to say that we are being lazy or sluggish—it is not our fault that we had to spend ten minutes standing in line at the bank. And while folding the laundry is a productive use of time, it frequently does not feel that way. So there is no reason you can't listen to podcasts or books on Audible while folding the laundry.

Now this is where our earlier discussion of tools comes in. Suppose you are reading through a book, and it is a "bucket book" of yours. Not *Moby Dick*, which you have already dispatched. This is a different bucket book, which means it is a book that you really ought to have read by this point in your life, but you inexplicably haven't done it yet.

Anna Karenina it is. This is not a book that you would necessarily just pick up and read "for fun," but you would enjoy having read it. As Mark Twain supposedly said, a classic is a book that nobody wants to read but everybody wants to have read. It's a classic, so you can probably get it on Kindle for 99 cents or something like that (or free from Project Gutenberg). You figure out that it is about 600 pages, and so you decide to read two pages a day, which gets you through that book in ten months. Not only is this grand and glorious, but here, today, in the line at the post office, you can take out your phone—because you have your Kindle app on your phone, right?—and knock out your two pages right there. But be careful about distractions. You can also watch cat videos while standing in line.

CHAPTER THIRTEEN

WORK AT A PACE
YOU CAN MAINTAIN

This chapter is not really a repetition of the previous one, but there is some overlap—of necessity. If you are plodding, you will notice that you are getting things done along the way. But as you are plodding, you will at some point recognize something else. You can go for a longer time. You can walk farther than you can sprint. The previous chapter was about plodding. This chapter is about plodding *and time.*

Working with your hair on fire is not really an effective long-term strategy. Urgency sometimes helps some people to concentrate, but usually it has the opposite effect. Choking on it is usually the way it goes.

The pace of work can be a problem two ways. One way is when the marathon runner starts out as though the race were a hundred-yard dash. Not surprisingly, he burns out after just a few minutes. Another trick, one that many learned in college by postponing the writing of the paper until the night before it was due, is the technique of walking the length of the marathon, and then bursting into a sprint for the last hundred yards. That usually doesn't work either.

Pascal observed somewhere that it is a mistake to think that we can do all of the time what we can do some of the time. Put another way, it is a mistake to think that your high points, or your fastest speeds, or your most productive moments, can simply be duplicated over and over again at will. All your most energetic moments cannot simply be placed end to end. Real life waxes and wanes, and a snapshot of your best moments cannot really be turned into a video. If you were really focused and able to do x, y, and z for a whole week running, it does not automatically follow that you could keep up that pace for a year. Or if you could do that for an hour, it does not mean you could do it for a week.

Perhaps you could, but it all depends. Methodical is what does the trick. An amazing amount of work can be accomplished through diligent plodding. But please note that I said plodding, not shuffling. There is a way of dragging your feet that doesn't really accomplish anything remarkable either. But simply placing one foot in front of the other, and doing so repeatedly, can get you across a continent within a reasonable amount of time.

The question to ask yourself is this: "For a dedicated worker, what is a reasonable average pace for this task?" In other words, what pace could be maintained through the undulations of very productive times and less productive times? What *average* can be maintained?

Other simple math problems suggest themselves. Taking our earlier example of a 365-page book, two pages a day gets the book read in six months. Those two pages take two to three minutes a day. I usually am reading several books at a time this way, which allows me to get through a hefty stack each year. Obviously, the thing to realize is how important those few minutes of reading are—important enough to make sure they happen every day. A day has 1,440 minutes in it, and so it might be hard to get into the habit of dedicating two or three of them to *Moby Dick*. But once you have established the pattern, it joins the ranks of the other daily (but brief) habits you might have—like putting on your socks, or brushing your teeth. If you decide that "this is simply going to happen," it is not that hard to find a minute to give to it.

This book was actually written by this method. While there were a few hectic times where it did not happen, I decided that I was going to chip away at this book by adding a hundred words to it every evening. When ten days have passed, there are a thousand words in the bank, which is roughly a chapter. If the first draft comes out at 20,000 words, then it took 200 days—at about five to ten minutes a day. I am not including in this count the time spent with the editors of Canon Press standing over me with the nine-tailed cat-o-suggested-edits.

I would submit that this is simply an effective way to use your time—more effective than what is frequently done, which is not using those small chunks of time productively. After all, a very common feature of the acknowledgment sections at the beginning of books is the part where the author thanks his long-suffering family for putting up with his surliness while he was Locked-in-the-Attic-in-Order-to-Write-the-Book, and for being willing to leave food by the door, tapping twice quietly, and then slipping silently away.

The thing to take away is that brief but daily routines are capable of accumulating a large amount of whatever the work product might be. A man could take out the trash every evening, and while out there quietly lay one brick, and after six months present his wife with a brick wall along the alley—something she never even knew she wanted.

CHAPTER FOURTEEN

PROGRESS AND DEPRAVITY

When it comes to modern conveniences, many Christians are confused about the relationship of their hot and cold running water to, say, the worldview of modernity, which is the outlook we inherited from the Enlightenment. If we reject the Enlightenment (and we should), does that mean we must be relegated to the grass huts like the green socialists are demanding? Put another way, is it possible to be modern without being a modernist? *Sure*, say I, and let me explain. As we have already shown, wealth is a gift from God, and pride is bequeathed to us from the devil. Is it clearer now?

The birth of the modern age, measured in terms of conveniences, technology, wealth, medical advances, and so on was largely a legacy of the Reformation. But the Bible teaches that whenever a gift is given, there will immediately be a temptation arising in our hearts to steal the glory and gratitude that should go to God alone. That temptation will say, fundamentally, that we owe none of this to God, and that we did it all ourselves. That *attitude* is what we call the Enlightenment. That is modernist hubris, technocratic arrogance, and purblind puffery.

Again, again, and again, wisdom from Deuteronomy:

"When thou hast eaten and art full, then thou shalt bless the LORD thy God for the good land which he hath given thee. Beware that thou forget not the LORD thy God, in not keeping his commandments, and his judgments, and his statutes, which I command thee this day: Lest . . . thou say in thine heart, My power and the might of mine hand hath gotten me this wealth. But thou shalt remember the LORD thy God: for it is he that giveth thee power to get wealth, that he may establish his covenant which he sware unto thy fathers, as it is this day" (Deut. 8:10-18).

This is the sinful pattern. God gives wealth, and man takes credit for it himself. If someone else comes along later and *blames* man for creating all this wealth and demands that we have ourselves a little "social justice" around here, he is just creating an extra layer of sedimentary silliness. And by this point, we don't need any extra layers of silliness.

The Enlightenment is not to be credited with Harvey's discovery of the circulation of the blood, Smith's discovery that no one man is capable of manufacturing a pin, Newton's discovery of what objects in motion tend to do, or Watts' admirable divvying up of energy into units of horsepower. God gave us all those things. We must thank *God* for them.

Seeing the inevitable abuses of wealth that follow after a humanistic grabbing of credit for it, and reacting by pulling away from the whole thing entirely, is simply foolish. If it is a good thing, as my smartphone is a good thing, then God is to be *thanked* for it. If it is a sinful thing, like thinking that man does things he can't ever do, then we should abandon our folly, repent of our sins, and return to the gospel of grace that undergirds all God's statutes and laws. And if you don't know where those passages are, you can look them up on your phone.

Jesus is the Lord of history, and this is why we don't need to be afraid of Twitter. Or Facebook. Or teenagers typing with their thumbs. Jesus is the Lord of history, which is why we don't need to worry about Google making us stupid.

Here's the thing. A common worry among modern sophisticates is that technology really is making us stupid. It would be better to say that technology when ignored or mismanaged makes us stupid, but this has always been the case with every form of wealth. And it is another way of saying that stupid gets stupider. There is nothing new about the modern world in this respect other than that more people are trying to cope with more blessings all at once than has ever happened before. That means more people are doing it poorly.

I say this as a lead-in to my expression of profound gratitude for my computers, my Bible software, my tablet, my phone, and all the other electronic servants God has given to me to manage. I don't do it very well yet, but I know that the opportunity to learn how to do it is an enormous blessing. I am a man who has ten thousand servants in his pocket, and thousands more in my study and office, and every year that goes by I am learning how to put more of them to productive labor. For this I am most grateful.

Don't mistake me. Google *does* make many of us stupid, but only in the same way that libraries have made us stupid for many centuries. Libraries make a handful of people really wise, and provide many others with artificial props for their footnotes.

Everywhere the human race goes, it drags a bell curve around with it. We put on airs because of where we are on the existing curve (or we feel bad because of where we are), but we fail to recognize that a blue-collar auto mechanic today is working with sophisticated electronics that would have completely stumped Aristotle on one of his good days. And one half of all medical doctors graduated in the lower half of their class, right?

We live in a time of tremendous innovation, development, and apparent chaos. There are many opportunities to worry about it all, and so I want to lay my cards on the table, if it were not completely obvious by this point, and talk about why I am excited about the future. This is going to sound funny, but I am excited about the future because I am a postmillennialist. And I am a postmillennialist because I am a Calvinist who believes that the sovereign God over all things is truly, inexhaustibly, and fiercely *good*. He keeps His promises. In addition to this, my Calvinism has helped me to understand the depravity of man and his ability to screw up pretty much anything.

So we need to remember that the eschatological future promised by the prophet Isaiah, and the future that was shaped by the Industrial Revolution and will continue to be shaped by the Digital Revolution, *are the same future*. I don't believe in an invisible spiritual future, shaped by the Holy

Spirit, full of sweetness and light, and an actual historical future shaped by the Devil, Halliburton, the Illuminati, and Murphy's law. The world, *this world*, is presently going where *Jesus* is taking it. So we should be wise, and stop worrying.

Part of being wise is that we do not forget the doctrine of sin. Sin is radical and deep, and capable of many cultural grotesqueries. We see them all the time, and we read about them all the time. Welcome to the spiritual war. Belief that we will win the war is not a denial of the reality of that war. My optimism is not of the kind that denies the existence of the battle. My optimism is of the kind that maintains that we are winning the battle.

To change the metaphor, to believe that the car is gassed up, running fine, and on the right road does not keep the kids from squabbling sinfully in the back seat. This means that every new development presents us with opportunities to sin, and, in a sinful world, the initial impulse *is* to sin. Wealth gotten by old-fashioned labor is sustained. Wealth gotten in the frothy way dissipates quickly (Prov. 13:11).

And so here is my central thesis, stated yet again: *technology in all its forms is a type of wealth*. The Bible contains no warnings about technology as such, but is crammed with warnings about the bias of wealth. Which way does wealth set us up? The Bible says that the wealthy are tempted to hubris, self-sufficiency, lack of concern for the poor, oppression, and the rest of that sorry lot. Wealth is a good thing, but it brings temptations. A lot of wealth is a lot of a good thing, but it brings with it a lot of temptations.

Say a man comes into wealth, and the first thing he does is join the swankiest country club. Not a good harbinger. The same thing is true of the guy who gains his wealth and then runs off to the inner city to join a new monastic community. That's a bad sign too.

It does not profit a man to gain the whole world and lose his soul in the process (Matt. 16:26). This remains true even if the world is in the process of gaining the world, but loses its soul on the way. Wealth is not a substitute savior. It is a good thing, a creational good, and it is one which we are tempted to set up as an idol (Eph. 5:5; Col. 3:5). Until the resurrection, wealth is a good thing which *always* tends to distract us from our love for Christ, and the task at hand.

CHAPTER FIFTEEN

ESCHATOLOGY

What we are seeing now with the multitude of silly applications of Facebook, Twitter, music downloads, research with Google books, and every new app you can think of is the response of the *nouveau riche* to windfall wealth—a response that is as old as dirt. There is nothing whatever that is new about this. There is nothing new under the sun.

We have always had worriers. Plato worried about the written word. At the birth of the modern era, others worried about the typeset word. Now we worry about the digitized word. And, let it be said, the worriers always have a point. They always have examples of actual folly in the early adapters that they can point to, and they are not making it up. But the fact that you are not making up the bad examples does not mean that you are fitting those bad examples into the right paradigm of interpretation.

A good example of an erudite worrier would be Neil Postman in *Amusing Ourselves to Death*. But for every book like that, given the propensity of Calvinists to worry excessively about the heart of man, I would recommend that you read three like Johnson's *Everything Bad is Good for You*, Postrel's *The Future and Its Enemies*, and Herman's *The Idea of Decline in Western History*. Why should Calvinists worry? In the collision between the sovereignty of Jesus in history, and the influence of sin in history, sin is the certain loser.

Now some will object that the books I have cited are not by believers. And I will point out in reply that things have gotten really bad when unbelievers can see what Jesus is doing more accurately than the believers can. When unbelievers by common grace are reading history right side up, why should we reject that in favor of believers who are reading their Bible upside down?

We worry about the course of history because we are not in control of it, and we like to pretend that this means no one is in control of it. But this follows not. Jesus is the Lord of history. He is the Lord of all *this*.

And that means that all will end well. It does not mean that everything ends well for everybody, for folly becomes apparent over time. In the long run, stupidity never works. You complain that some stupid teenager is exhilarated because he has twenty-eight superficial "friends" on Facebook. Okay, that's dumb, but how is it different from our practice of writing old-fashioned letters to a mortal enemy, making sure the letter begins with a term of endearment, "Dear . . ." *Dear*?

Keep moving, people. Nothing to see here. Nothing new here. Nothing new under the sun. Some are wise, and many are (comparatively) foolish. The only question before us now is whether or not we will be among the wise or the foolish. Carping criticism from outside, from some kind of Unabomber cabin, is not an effective response. It is not wise—even if you are gracious enough to write from a Wendell Berry cabin instead.

Jesus is the Word, and by His Incarnation He has sanctified the right use of words for all time. The Internet has given us a torrent of words—what else is new? And the fact that the torrent has increased so much should fill us with a sense of exhilaration. Our responsibility as people of the Word is to give ourselves to the study and practice of how all this can be used wisely.

Christians are those who worship the Father through the Word, and consequently we are also people of words. The digital earthquake deep underneath the Pacific has resulted in a tsunami that is headed for Seattle. That is a problem . . . for Seattle. But it is not a problem for the fish. Christians are logocentric, people of words. Why should we be bothered by a tsunami of words? This is where we swim.

My optimism about tools and technology is, at bottom, an optimism about the future history of the world. And that, in its turn, is an optimism that is grounded on the fact that at the darkest point of human history, God in the flesh was crucified by arrogant sinners, by all the important people. Three days after that, the Lord came back from the dead. That means that the old world has been overthrown. How could that world not be overthrown? That world is dead because its only power was death, and we serve a Lord who went into death's maw, and then came out again. That is the ultimate plot turn. That is the central fact of all human history.

"For God sent not his Son into the world to condemn the world; but that the world through him might be saved" (John 3:17).

The mission given to the Lord Jesus was that of saving the world. And He has laid the foundation of that salvation in His death, burial, and resurrection, and in the two thousand years since that time, the Spirit He poured out on the Church has been working through all human cultures, the way leaven works through the loaf. Not only are multitudes of individuals saved, but churches are planted, and the Kingdom grows and expands. The lordship of Christ is honored when a people turns to Christ, and His authority is extended over them. The Great Commission says that we are to disciple the nations. The verb is disciple and the direct object of that verb is nations, the *ethnoi*. We disciple them by baptizing them, and teaching them to obey everything Jesus commanded. His authority extends over all of life.

Now this means that when a culture turns to Christ, His authority extends past their hearts. His authority extends over their laws, their movies, their songs, and their screwdrivers. Those screwdrivers, in case you missed the implication, are a basic item in their repository of tools. And because His authority is over all of us, it is also over all of our tools, from the bottom of the tool chest to the very top of it. And not only so, but Jesus is Lord of history, which means His authority extends from Adam's first honeycomb stick, at the beginning, down to the last tool invented, which will probably be something like a transport barge for hauling radioactive waste to be dumped into the sun. It'll be totally safe. We did tests and everything.

CHAPTER SIXTEEN

THE NEW MEDIA

If your use of Twitter is limited to informing all your followers that you are rummaging in the fridge for some Dr. Pepper at two a.m., then sure, quit that. But suppose you tell your followers that poverty and shame come to the one who refuses instruction, what now? How is that an abuse of Twitter? It is a godly word. And we can't complain that biblical wisdom doesn't really come in small packages like that because an entire book of the Bible is made up of small packages like that. You could tweet a proverb a day, and it would be a long time before you were done.

The apostle Paul wrote letters, and used the available technologies to get them delivered—whether ships, or Roman roads, or carts, or parchments, or pens. He would have preferred to have been with the Galatians in person, but he used technology to close the gap. The Reformation began in 1517, and the moveable type printing press was invented a short time before that, somewhere around 1450. It is hard for us to envision what we know as the Reformation without the technology of printing and printed editions of books.

When the apostles preached in the ancient cities of the Roman Empire, they went and preached *where the people were.* If the people were congregated in the forum, then that is where the evangelists went. If they were gathered on Mars Hill, then no one should have been shocked when the apostle Paul arrived there with his message. When the bank robber Willie Sutton was asked why he robbed banks, his reply was "Because that's where the money is." Christians should go with our life-transforming message, and where should we go? *Where the people are.* And where people gather today is online. And when we go there, we should not go to them with a truncated gospel. Rather, we must proclaim a gospel that encompasses everything—all of Christ for all of life.

What do I mean by a truncated gospel? I mean a gospel that restricts itself to telling people how to get into Heaven when they die. That is important enough, because missing Heaven is not a trifle, and so that is frequently where we should start. But if we stop there, then we are not being faithful to the fullness of the biblical gospel.

One debate among some evangelicals is over whether Christ can be accepted as Savior only, or whether He must be accepted as Savior and Lord. Those who insist, rightly, that the basic Christian confession is *Jesus is Lord* do well. But we also have to make sure not to understand *that* in a truncated way.

A truncated view of Christ's lordship is one that limits it to His authority over my personal life. A person taking this view says, again rightly, that Christ cannot be received on an installment plan, first as Savior and then, five years later, as Lord. But even here, what is frequently being asserted is that Jesus needs to be Lord of a man's life.

And of course that is true. But we are not working from the bottom up. We proclaim the lordship of Christ over everything, and we do so, not because we have invited Him into our hearts, but rather because He rose from the dead, ascended into the presence of the Ancient of Days, and was given a universal and cosmic authority (Dan. 7:13-14). In the Great Commission, Jesus said that all authority in Heaven and on earth had been given to Him. On *that* basis, we were supposed to go out and disciple the nations.

Another way of thinking about this is that we are not conducting a presidential campaign, trying to get as many people as possible to vote for Jesus, so that if we are successful, then He can assume a position of authority. No, His position is already one of a conquering monarch, and He is already on the throne. He has been seated on the throne of a cosmic empire, and our task is to announce this already accomplished coronation to all the people in the outlying villages.

And so we are summoning men to bow before Him in response to the authority He has. We are not trying to gather up authority for Him from the people in order to grant Him the right to do anything He wants. The Kingdom of God is not a democracy.

Jesus is already Lord of those who recognize it, and He is already Lord of those who refuse to recognize it. This means that the authority of Jesus Christ, right now and not later, currently extends over Facebook, Google, and Twitter. He is the Lord of all the ones and zeroes. He is the Lord of the microprocessor. He is the Lord of the dark web. He is the Lord of all silicon, and the sand it rode in on. He is the Lord of Amazon, and the Lord of that little indie bookstore around the corner. He is the Lord of all our military drones, and all our delivery drones. He is the Lord of all of our great ones, and He is the Lord of the municipal dogcatchers.

So wherever people are, Christians should be right there, with all our work, talking about the *Lord*. You know, *the* Lord. The Lord over all of *this*. This means the new media is a great place to declare that the new media has not created any new gods, and is not a god itself, but rather is under the authority of the one who bound Satan before taking all of his stuff (Lk. 11:21-22). Included in the stuff taken was all of our tech equipment. It belongs to Jesus now.

Jesus is the Lord of history, and that means He is the Lord of history up to this point. He is governing all things in such a way as to bring this planet to a glorious conclusion. The history of the world, when it is finally written, will be seen as a comedy, concluding with a great wedding. It will not conclude as a tragedy. So as the Lord steers the ship of human history into the safe harbor of the New Jerusalem, sailing alongside the ships of Tarshish, we may look around us and see that He is not just bringing *us* into harbor, but also bringing the cargo and the tools.

ACKNOWLEDGMENTS,

Accomplishments,

and Deft Avoidance of the Humblebrag

One of the things the editors of this book would like is some mention of the various projects and accomplishments that help to qualify me as someone with a right to write about productivity. At the same time, I have a spiritual interest in not—as the apostle Paul once put it so pithily—tooting my own horn. Fortunately, I think I figured out a couple of ways to satisfy all the above, which in itself is another accomplishment that really should be mentioned.

There are two kinds of accomplishments that I could point to. One would be the founding of organizations or institutions, and the other would be personal output, as in writing books and things.

With regard to starting things, the trick here is to act like you know what you're doing, make the decision to "go for it," and then God sends capable people to help you implement the vision. What you need to do is make the call, and then go stand on the Cliff of Leadership that overlooks the Ocean of Possibilities, in order to stare at the remote horizon with a steely gaze. God then lays a burden on the hearts of various competent sorts to go help that crazy man. Something very much like this has happened to me numerous times. So on the one hand, I could be plausibly credited with founding numerous institutions—Open Door Crisis Pregnancy Center (now CareNet of the Palouse), Logos School, New St. Andrews College, Greyfriars' Hall, the Association of Classical and Christian Schools, the Communion of Reformed Evangelical Churches, Canon Press, *Credenda Agenda* magazine, and Blog & Mablog. On the other hand, it is crucial to highlight my profound gratitude to God for Roy Atwood, Doug Jones, Tom Garfield, Patch Blakey, Gene Helsel, Brett Baker, Randy Booth, Joost Nixon, Larry Stephenson, and (as you might guess) numerous others. Had God not sent them around, the world would have seen a rather gaudy display of my ongoing administrative skills, which would have put them in mind of the crash of the Hindenburg.

When it comes to personal output, I have to credit my father for two crucial lessons that I learned from him, almost important enough to warrant a separate appendix of their own. The first was the importance of inductive study of the Bible, which is to say, asking questions of the text that can actually be answered *from the text*. I remember one episode vividly. When I was in junior high, my father had started a junior high Bible study with the intention of teaching us how to interrogate the text, and not one another, or our own unreliable hearts. We were all sitting around in a circle, open Bibles on our laps, and my father, as the one leading the study, asked us a question. We all sat there, looking at him, for was he not the teacher? And he said, "The answer's not on my forehead." We were learning the importance of what the apostle Paul said in another setting, which is to not "go beyond what is written" (1 Cor. 4:6). The Scriptures are the repository of all the essential wisdom that God wants us to have, and my father taught me, whenever I have a question, to turn to the text first. To the law and the testimony. Back to the text.

The second lesson built on the first. I forget what the occasion was when I learned this from him, but it has stayed with me over numerous years. He said, "Whenever you run out of things to say, go on to the next verse." If you know how to extract the sense of the text, and there is always another text waiting, the end result is that there is always something edifying to say. And because much of the Christian world has not been taught how to read, and where to go next, it strikes them as a marvel when it happens. Where do you get these things? The answer is fundamentally as basic as "the next verse."

I also have to acknowledge God's goodness to me in my family. My wife Nancy is a wise and gracious Christian woman, one who has been on the same page with me since we first met, and who has led numerous book and Bible studies for women and written numerous books. She is a student of the Word and a student of the Puritans, and is a worthy Puritan herself. I have three children and seventeen grandchildren, all of whom love the Lord. My children are married to capable and godly Christians who match them in unbelievable fruitfulness. All of them get the vision, and all of them love it. This is, to use the words of the psalmist, a force multiplier (Ps. 127:5). It ties in with what I said earlier about seeking to have God bless your labors, and the central labor you should want Him to bless is your labor as a father. If that is blessed, your own productivity is multiplied. If it is not, the erosion is a real sorrow.

And so these acknowledgments are at bottom an acknowledgement that all worthwhile kingdom work is done by numerous citizens of that Kingdom. No one person is responsible for all of it, and while some parts of the body are more *visible* than others, it is the body that actually accomplishes what God is doing through them. One part of the body has no business boasting over the other parts of the body. Charles de Gaulle put it memorably when he said that graveyards are full of indispensable men.